THE ❧ ❧ ❧ ❧ ❧ GOLDEN FLOWER

Comte de Gobineau

THE ❧ ❧ ❧ ❧ ❧ GOLDEN FLOWER

BY

ARTHUR, COUNT GOBINEAU

TRANSLATED FROM THE FRENCH, AND
WITH AN INTRODUCTION BY
BEN RAY REDMAN

Essay Index Reprint Series

BOOKS FOR LIBRARIES PRESS
FREEPORT, NEW YORK

41990

First Published 1924
Reprinted 1968

LIBRARY OF CONGRESS CATALOG CARD NUMBER:
68-54347

PRINTED IN THE UNITED STATES OF AMERICA

INTRODUCTION

THE justification for burdening this small book with an Introduction is twofold, and one that amounts virtually to a necessity. Both the author and his book furnish cause: in the first place, Count Gobineau, although now the recipient of belated eulogy and cult-worship in Germany and France, is still unknown by more than name to the generality of cultivated American readers, despite the fact that for some years two of his principal works have been obtainable here in translation; in the second place, "The Golden Flower" can be properly appreciated only if its connection with another of Gobineau's books is understood. From the nature of the case, then, it is evident that the primary function of the required Introduction

is expository rather than critical. If it
serves, additionally, to throw into a clear
light the significance of ' "The Golden
Flower," as viewed in relation to Gobineau's earlier writings, it will have
accomplished its whole purpose.

Logically the author takes precedence
of his book, and he is a man who might
well tempt the biographer. Joseph Arthur,
Comte de Gobineau, was a diplomat by
profession and long practice; by avocation
he was philosopher, historian, archæ-
ologist, Orientalist, novelist, poet, and
sculptor. Above all, and in the broadest
meaning of the term, he was a man of
letters, passionately, persistently, to the
end of his life. So he takes his place in
that distinguished line of gifted Frenchmen who have successfully combined
diplomacy with literature. This philosopher who represented his nation in many
lands found time in the midst of official
duties to compose a score and more of
books that might well stand as monument

to a lifetime devoted exclusively to writing. Count Gobineau's diplomatic efforts were rewarded by the hostility of bureaucrats who prematurely put a close to his career; his books were welcomed by a vast silence, broken by only a few isolated hails of recognition. Not until twenty years after his death did his countrymen discover what kind of man he really was; now that he has been dead for more than forty years, he is accorded praise and veneration perhaps beyond his due. Here, surely, ready to the biographer's hand, are the materials for a most instructive comedy of justice.

Since 1913, a fairly detailed account of Gobineau's life has been available in Dr. Oscar Levy's capable Introduction to the English translation of "The Renaissance." The essential facts are all there; but a brief biographical sketch is desirable here, and this will involve the correction of certain dates set down by Dr. Levy, and the mention of various facts not included in his account.

Gobineau was born at Ville d'Avray, on July 14th, 1816; he died at Turin, on October 13th, 1882. His family was Royalist, and Joseph Arthur never deviated from the aristocratic ideals that must have been commended to him in his boyhood. In 1830, young Gobineau spent several months traveling through Germany with his mother, after which he entered a Swiss school where the courses were conducted in German. It is worthy of note that his first contacts with Teutonic culture were made at an impressionable age, and it is notable also that at this time he developed the passionate interest in Oriental languages which he was never to abandon. Joining his father at Lorient, in 1832, he continued his Oriental studies and essayed expression in verse. His father, it appears, was quite impecunious, so in 1835 the youth journeyed to Paris, with fifty francs in his pocket, to establish himself in the household of his uncle Thibault-Joseph, a man of some wealth, a fiery defender of the old régime, and an exceedingly eccentric character.

For the next thirteen years Gobineau devoted himself to a career of study and writing. A minor position in the postal department yielded him a small income, but his chief activities were those of any young man who is attempting to win a foothold in the journalistic and literary world of a metropolis. His first published essay—significantly enough a study of the condottiere Alviano—appeared in *Unité*, in 1841. After that his political articles, reviews, literary studies, prose, and verse found their way into an increasing number of periodicals: he contributed to the *Revue des Deux Mondes*, *La Quotidienne*, the *Revue de Paris*, *Le Commerce*, the *Revue Nouvelle*, the *Journal des Debats*, and other organs of opinion and literature. He was a promising young writer in a city of promising young writers; but he was differentiated from the herd by his exceptional intelligence and his industry as a student.

His first book, *Les Adieux de Don Juan*, was published in 1844, and two years later he married Gabrielle-Clémence Monerot. A play by Gobineau was accepted by the Comédie Française in 1848, but the February Revolution of that fateful year prevented its production. The birth of his first daughter in September marked the close of a clear-cut period in his life. He was on the threshold of a very different scene.

During his Parisian activities, Gobineau had come to know the gifted Alexis de Tocqueville, mouthpiece of orthodox liberalism and imitator of Montesquieu. The "shortest and least sanguinary" of French revolutions thrust this theorist into public office, first as Vice President of the Assembly, and then as Minister of Foreign Affairs. Tocqueville occupied this latter post for a few months only, but he held it long enough to make Count Gobineau his chief of cabinet, in June, 1849, and thus launch him on a diplomatic career that continued until a few years before his death. Ironical as it is that Gobineau should owe his posthumous fame chiefly to the efforts of Richard Wagner, a man whose mind was the antithesis of his own, it is equally ironical that his life should have been so fateful directed by Tocqueville, who was separated from him intellectually by an impassable abyss.

When Tocqueville retired from office, the Count continued in official favor, and in November, 1849, he was appointed first secretary to the legation at Berne. Before two years had passed, he went to Hanover as chargé d'affaires, and in January, 1854, he became first secretary at Frankfort. It was during this period that he composed his "Essay on the Inequality of the Human Races," for which the groundwork had been laid during the long years in Paris, and which appeared in two parts, in 1853 and 1855. As the Essay has been generally considered the capital work of Gobineau's life, and as his posthumous influence and fame rise from this book, an explanatory digression is necessary at this point.

The Essay attempted no less than to account for the destinies of races, it sought to subject an infinitely multifarious mass of historical phenomena to a single force, racial law. To blood alone all fates were traceable: climate, religion, all the forces of environment, were ignored by Gobineau. If Taine, in his analysis of culture, laid exclusive emphasis on *milieu*, Gobineau, in his analysis of racial destinies, went to the opposite extreme. And he was extreme, surely, in the application of his law, for he dogmatically stated that one race, and one race only, had been capable of creating a true civilization. That race was the Aryan, and in it had reposed all hope of man's perfectibility: but, as that race had ruined itself by adulteration of its pure blood, mankind was doomed. The one force for salvation had destroyed itself; the true prophet must be a prophet of despair.

There is no need to point out here the

fallacies of this thesis; that service has been performed by many writers, and the American reader will find Dr. Levy's analysis of the Essay thoroughly satisfactory. Count Gobineau buttressed his theory with masses of erudition quarried from many fields of scholarship; but he failed, as every thinker must fail who seeks in a single factor the sole key to multiplex phenomena. The "system" of historical Aryanism, which Gobineau was the first to set forth in completeness, was destined to exert extensive influence; but this system, was conceived on the very eve of the birth of a still greater system that was to dominate the thought of the late nineteenth century. And "The Golden Flower" furnishes conclusive proof that Gobineau was not blind to the light of a new dawn. Of this more later.

In 1855, with the Crimean War in full swing, the Count set out for Persia, with his wife and daughter, to occupy the post of first secretary at Teheran. This same

year was marked by the death of his uncle,
and by the publication of the second part
of his Essay. 1858 saw Gobineau back in
France, his second daughter having been
born during the preceding year, and *Trois
Ans en Asie* (1859) appeared as the fruit
of the author's first sojourn in Persia.
Shortly after his return, he published
Lectures des Textes Cunéiformes; in the
same year, his father died.

After receiving a nomination as first
secretary to China, a post that he never
filled, the Count sailed for Newfoundland,
in 1859, to assist in the settlement of
fishery rights. *Voyage à Terre-Neuve* was
the literary product of this brief journey.
June of the next year found him delegated
to the international commission which was
dealing with the annexation of Savoy;
after which he was appointed Minister to
Persia, and in 1861 he again set out for the
land which interested him so deeply, where
he spent two more years in an attempt to
strengthen the then feeble French influ-

ence. Returning on leave from Persia, in 1863, the Count was named Minister to Greece in the following year; an appointment for which he had no liking, as his desires had fastened on Constantinople. But to Athens he went, and during the several years spent in that city he labored unremittingly at letters; his second visit to Persia had made possible *Les Religions et les philosophies dans l'Asie centrale* (1865), and shortly after his departure for Brazil, as Minister, in 1869, appeared his *Histoires des Perses* and his collection of poems, *L'Aphroessa.*

Brazil was for Gobineau an exile that was cheered only by the friendship of another lonely man, the imperial exile Dom Pedro. It was a brief banishment, however, for in 1870 the Count was back in France, ready to act, during the war, as Mayor of Trye, his uncle's legacy having enabled him to purchase the chateau of Trye-en-Vexin. During the Commune he was in Paris, and later at Versailles.

In 1872, he went to Stockholm as Minister, and it was there that he composed *La Renaissance*, published in 1877, with which we are here especially concerned. There, too, he wrote *Les Pléiades*, a philosophic novel, and it was toward the end of his stay there that his *Nouvelles Asiatiques* appeared. Gobineau left Stockholm to journey through Europe with his friend Dom Pedro, and it was in Rome, on his way home, in November, 1876, that he first met Richard Wagner.

Early in the next year, Count Gobineau was prematurely retired by a democratic bureaucracy that had no further use for the aristocratic philosopher. The last years of his life were undoubtedly darkened by this injustice, while, curiously enough, they were lighted by his association with the composer of *Parsifal*, with whom Nietzsche had just definitely broken, and with whom the influencer of Nietzsche could have held nothing intellectually in common. Indeed, this friendship, fateful in its consequences, was stranger than the understanding which existed between Giovanni de' Medici and Guliano della Rovere, at which, in the pages of this book, Gobineau himself marvels. Trips to Italy, visits to Bayreuth, sculpture, and a small portion of belated fame in Germany, resulting from Wagner's enthusiasm, marked Gobineau's last days. In 1882 he went to Italy for the last time; he died suddenly in Turin as he was about to take the train for Pisa.

Such was the life of Count Gobineau, a life spent dutifully in the service of his country, but primarily consecrated to the work of literature. His many books fell almost unheeded from the press: Tocqueville was mightily disturbed by the thesis of the Essay, and did not "wish to believe" that there was truth in it; Renan found cause to praise the Count's Oriental studies; and that fiery soldier of Catholicism, Barbey d'Aurevilley unbent to admire the erudition and spirit of the author of *Les Pléiades*. But these readers were few, and the books served chiefly to arouse suspicion in official circles. I see no reason to agree with Gobineau's grandson that there was a conspiracy of silence: French men of letters were simply, for the most part, unaware of the Count's existence. Gobineau died, in a foreign land, in the care of strangers, and his countrymen knew him not.

Years passed; and then, about 1898, a whisper slipped across the Rhine that the Germans had discovered a great French author, that a society had been instituted at Freiburg-ins-Breisgau for the translation, publication, and dissemination of his works. Paris was puzzled, and critical curiosity, now awakened, began to run down odd volumes by the neglected writer: Frenchmen read these books, they were thrilled, and they recorded their reaction at length and in no uncertain terms. The French discovery of Gobineau commenced with the beginning of the century, and

since then books, articles, and biographical
sketches, dealing with all phases of the
Count's activity and thought, have piled
themselves up at a dizzy rate, until now a
French Gobineau cult takes its stand
proudly beside that larger group which
does worship at the shrine of Henri
Beyle. Justice at last, and perhaps something more than justice, has been done.

This consummation resulted directly
from the chance meeting with Richard
Wagner, for the German composer, having
read the Essay, and having happily failed
to understand its meaning and its impli-
cations, set out to establish the author's
fame in Germany. For this purpose, the
demigod of Bayreuth delegated one of his
most enthusiastic disciples, Professor Lug-
wig Schemann, to the task of translation
and proselytism, and so thoroughly did the
good Professor do his work that Gobineau
became the god of a society and the in-
spirer of a nation. Dr. Levy has analysed
at some length the German failure to

understand Gobineau which permitted the Germans to clasp him to their heart, and to the reader I recommend Dr. Levy on this point. Briefly, the Germans mistook Gobineau's "exaggerated praise of the German conqueror tribes" for "praise of the modern German citizen," for whom he had a supreme contempt; so, too, they misunderstood the temper of his anti-Semitism, and in such mistakes and such misunderstandings have the Chamberlains, the Reventlows and the Hitlers found nourishment.

It is notable that, while the Count was suffering neglect in France, a translation of his Essay was published in Philadelphia only one year after the appearance of its second part. The fact particularly deserves mention because the reception accorded a subsequent English translation indicated that even avowed Gobinistes were ignorant of this volume. It was published at the direction of a certain H. Hotz, a slave owner, and at least one per-

son in the United States anticipated
Germany in the feat of misunderstanding
Gobineau. There is no way of estimating
how many Americans read this book—
dedicated to "The Statesmen of America"
—or what they thought of it; but Hotz, at
least, believed he had found an apologist
for slavery. So here again the Count's
reception was founded on misapprehension,
and he could remark cynically, when
informed of Hotz' desire to publish an
expurgated translation: "Our friends the
Americans think that I am encouraging
them to lynch their negroes, but they cannot abide that part of my book which
really concerns them. . . ."

We must turn now to "The Renaissance," for the book here translated is,
as originally conceived, an integral part
of that drama. "The Golden Flower"
consists of five historical essays, each
designated to serve as preface to one of the
five parts composing Count Gobineau's

historic play, and each casting new light upon a production that must some day be considered the Count's masterpiece. These prefaces were not included in the volume published in 1877; precisely why we are not sure, but it seems that the publisher, fearing too bulky a work, was probably responsible. Whatever the cause, the papers lay in manuscript in the little Gobineau Museum at Strasbourg, until the indefatigable Schemann published them in 1918. In 1924, they appeared in France.

Gobineau's drama, the values of which the candid critic must admit are more historical than dramatic, is cast in a form that might well have served as partial model for Thomas Hardy's "The Dynasts" had the English poet ever read the Frenchman's work. The Count is content to seek expression within the range of prose, but his structure and his choice of incident are comparable to Hardy's. A great epoch is revealed by a succession of illuminated scenes, some long, some brief, some peopled by persons of enduring eminence, some made animate by anonymous representatives of the masses. The dancing, penetrating light of the author's intelligence shifts rapidly, throwing contrasting scenes into juxtaposition, illumining high places and low levels to the end that a whole age may be revealed. A single man, in whom some phase of the Renaissance is incarnate, dominates each portion of the drama.

First there is Savonarola, the prophet, the God-inspired preacher, who fought desperately against the Time Spirit and sought to turn the sun back in its course, the embodiment of reactionism, the very antithesis of all that the Italian Renaissance was striving toward, one of the greatest of that host that Heine calls "the black brood of monks." Savonarola thundered in the Cathedral of Florence, and for an instant imposed his reforms upon the people; but the march of the age bore him down and swept over him.

Then there is Cesare Borgia, supreme

representative of the Nietzchean master-
morality, a man ignoring good and evil,
concerned solely with the accomplishment
of his own purposes, bending to that task,
great gifts and great energies who "stalked
through central Italy just as Cortez some
years later was to march across Mexico";
and who furnished Machiavelli with a hero
for his *Principe*. But, as the worthy Niccolo
demonstrates, the life of Cesare reveals
the instability of *fortuna;* and fortune
crushed the master-moralist at the last.

In Julius II we find a Pope who admir-
ably represents the immense vigor, courage, restlessness, and ambition of the
Renaissance. "In the general seething,
he seethed more then any other . . .
Scrupulous he was not; but who was?"
Yet Guliano della Rovere was more
scrupulous that the Borgias, in his private
relations if not in public affairs. Matters
of state revealed him as hard and as
flexible as steel: he formed an alliance with
the French, he brought them into Italy, he

turned upon them and drove them out again; it was all for the greater glory of the Church and of Italy. He was one of a line of formidable Papal politicians, but his policies, calculated to consolidate the power that he administered, served really to further the ruin of his country; his dealings with Charles VIII, the League of Cambray, his employment of the Swiss mercenaries, all served to introduce destructive forces into Italy. It is in the world of art and letters that his place is assured, and Count Gobineau pays him the proper tribute when he writes "thus it is that this haughty and turbulent pontiff was assuredly the most effective among the protectors of the arts, just as the time in which he reigned was the true period of expansion of the genius of the Renaissance."

Giovanni de' Medici, second son of Lorenzo the Magnificent, who succeeded Julius II as Leo X, was made of very different stuff from that which composed the

Pontifice terribile. Here we find a metal
softer than steel. Squandering the revenues of the Papacy on the luxuries and the
arts that he adored, he has won everlasting
fame for himself as a golden patron; but
his subtle brain, however cunning in
intrigue, however acute in artistic per-
ceptions, moved in a narrow circle as compared to the vast range of Julius' imagination. With Leo, the Medici took precedence of the Church and Italy, the old
nepotism was restored; the langorous
twilight of the Renaissance was setting in,
magnificent ambitions and great crimes
were giving way to mean desires and petty
sins. The spacious days were past.

Michael Angelo, who moves through the
five acts, and who gives his name to the
last, stands as the incarnation of all that
was purest, most vigorous and most enduring in the Italian Renaissance. While
Popes were setting poisoned wine before
their beloved Cardinals, while mobs were
cowering in terror beneath the eloquence

of Savonarola, while these same mobs were jeering at the awful execution of the great Dominican, while Dukes and Popes were inviting foreign armies to trample under foot Italian soil, while the clergy slumbered in sensual content and while the Church wasted resources drawn from the whole world, Michael Angelo and artists of the same spirit if with less genius were making sure the immortality of their age. In Michael Angelo the miracle of the Renaissance took shape. With justice could Gobineau make him say: "We are bequeathing a great legacy, great examples. . . . The earth is richer than it was before our coming. . . . What is to disappear will not disappear altogether. . . . The fields can rest and remain fallow for a while; the seed is in the clods. The fog may spread and the grey and watery sky become covered with mist and rain; but the sun is above. . . . Who knows what will come again."

These, then, are the five men whom

Gobineau selected as the dominating fig-
ures of his drama, a drama peopled by a
host of characters who will live so long as
history endures. The essays here translated are intended to set forth the circum-
stances that made these men's actions
possible, and to illuminate the historic
scenes in which they played their rôles.
Each essay sets the stage for the act it was
intended to precede. As an introduction
to "The Renaissance," this book is in-
valuable; as a commentary on that drama
it is no less important. But it will be
found to fulfill a greater function, for it
is a serviceable key to the epoch itself.

To all men the Italian Renaissance is
one of the most stirring and fascinating
periods of history, but to Count Gobineau
this age offered an especial appeal. Lud-
wig Schemann has written: "Never, perhaps, has the abyss between æsthetics
and politics, between appearance and
being, between heart and mind, been so
great." It was this contrast that fired

Gobineau's thought. Here, if ever, the philosopher could study the inconsistencies of the animal man in their most exaggerated form. This age in which the most beautiful flowers of art sprang from a bed of moral corruption and intellectual anarchy can never cease to provoke the thinker and the historian. Men turned from beauty to butchery with complacent satisfaction; they left a lamp burning before a bust of Plato while they hearkened to warnings of the wrath to come in the cathedral of Florence. The forces of antiquity were acting potently upon men's minds; meanwhile, in the north, a new civilization was arising and bearing down upon the south.

There is no cause for wonder that Count Gobineau, the passionate student of mankind, should have found inspiration in this terrible and fruitful epoch, lighted at once by the flames of genius and of the funeral pyre. What does demand explanation is the relation that his concep-

tion of the Renaissance bears to the
"system" first expressed in his famous
Essay and thereafter many times reiter-
ated. The common critical dictum has
been that Gobineau, despite the multifarious forms of his expression, was un-
swervingly faithful to one thesis. Edouard
Schuré says that he was "all his life the
paladin of one idea." This idea, as we
know, was that one race alone was capable
of producing a real civilization, that this
race had ruined itself by miscegenation,
and that civilization was therefore doomed.

When we turn from this narrow, dogmatic thesis to "The Golden Flower,"
what do we find? A conception of history
that is a thousand times broader, a thousand times more profound. In the opening
pages is expounded the theory that civilization is recurrent: all societies must pass
through phases inevitable to life: birth,
adolescence, maturity, senescence, and
death. But the death of anything is not
that terrible end of which Gobineau

dreamed in his Essay, it is simply "the commencement of its appropriation to new states." The terror of death, the terror of decay, can find no place in this conception. From the detritus of Greek civilization, Gobineau sees arise the age of Augustus; from the detritus of all antiquity, he witnesses the birth of the Renaissance. Was the age of Rome better or worse than that of Greece? Gobineau cannot say; he is content to say that it was different. Here is the broadest of historical conceptions, far indeed from the narrow "system" of Aryanism. There can be no forecast of inevitable doom, for in death there is new life.

The definite transformation of Gobineau's thought is clear, there is no dodging it. Where shall we find the cause? In the appearance of that mightier system at which I hinted earlier. When Gobineau published his Essay, Darwin's first great work was four years from completion; when he composed "The Renaissance,"

ILLUSTRATIONS

PART I

SAVONAROLA

Savonarola

O F the earth inhabited by man, man
in the beginning had no very clear
idea. He gazed upon the vast seas that
were sometimes barriers, sometimes high-
ways, and he saw that they separated or
united the nations which were scattered
over the shores of the continents. At first
man named these vast seas sterile. He
was fear stricken by their tempests, by
those mountains of surging water that the
winds raise, lash, and shatter in terrifying
agitation; and had not the greatest of
poets, smitten by sacred terror, stated
that nothing good could come forth from
this fierce turbulence? But, after Homer,
other lyres grew more learned: beneath the
anger of Neptune, the caprices of Amphi-
tryon, the cruel humors of the Nereides

3

and the abrupt transformations of Proteus,
they hymned the opulence of Ocean, its
crystal caverns pearl incrusted, the coral
that grew about its rocks, the amber that
floated amid its ice; and above all, beyond
all, from the bosom of its bluish tide, from
its thick, white, scintillating, flaky foam,
wise men had seen arise the peerless ap-
parition of triumphant Aphrodite. Later,
when imagination found itself too withered
and too old to carry on this cult of
youthful imagery, what is called science
still recognized that these transplendent
symbols bodied forth the truth, and that,
in fact, the salty sea, the brackish sea, the
sea of dark waters, charged with multiple
substances, was the depository of life-
germs, and that, far from meriting the
antique reproach of sterility, it magnifi-
cently surpassed in fecund activity the
green surface of the planet.

The moral world, in whose breast are
born and develop movements of another
kind, presents a spectacle similar to that

HIERONYMI·FERRARIENSIS·ADEO·
*MISSI·PROPHETÆ·EFFIGIES·

Fra Girolamo Savonarola

of the land and the enveloping ocean. It
puts forth the same appearances, it ends
in the same contradictions between what
seems and what is. Considering it only
in the mass, it displays above the accumulated waves of time a certain number of
epochs that may be compared to continents. The portions that are high, dis-
closed and clearly seen, illumined by the
sun, and considered of all ages especially
worthy of interest, are few in number; they
occupy but scant space in the expanse of
the ages. To enumerate them is a quickly
finished task. There is the epoch in which
Pericles ruled; there is the opulent period
of the Selucidæ and of the Ptolemies.
Then appears the Roman splendor under
Augustus; this ends with the Antonines,
and a great gulf separates it from the
period in which Christian theology, inspiring the feudal hierarchy, produced the
genius of the twelfth and thirteenth centuries of our era. At this point the ascent
halts anew; like a smoking lamp, history

gradually dims its light and is enveloped in shadows; it seems ready to flicker out, and it finds no new life until the second half of the fifteenth century.

During the periods that lie between these luminous moments, the days, the stream of days, the stream of facts, flow on, troubled and indistinct; this is the sterile sea, the Homeric bard would say again. But no! It is the fecund sea, stirring in its depths, bearing on its surface the germs of future things, leaving to float humbly upon the face of its waters that interlaced vegetation, devoid of brilliance but ever constant, that upholds amid tufted leaves, plated upon the sombre cloth, the golden flowers, great marvels of human vitality. For they are golden flowers, those splendid times in which men built the Parthenon, the Capitol, the cathedrals of Beauvais and of Amiens, and when all Italy was ablaze with life, with myriad colors, with wit, intelligence, with genius and with beauty.

These are golden flowers; glitteringly they swim and expand above the murmurous depths of days that have produced them and the mass of animated substance whence they have issued. These are golden flowers, like unto that mystic lotus of Indian wisdom, which, having opened into throbbing life upon a sea churned by celestial powers, carries in the midst of its petals a seated god who majestically contemplates the world that is illumined by light darting from his brow.

But while the golden flower is thus born of dark humidity, of the viscous coherence of latent fecundity, many other creatures come forth from the same source; these cling to its sides, thrust themselves against it, climb over it, cluster together, work against it, and finally achieve its destruction in precisely the same fashion that, in the world of nature, the winds, glaciers, volcanoes, currents, voracious animals, insects, worms, and minuscule monsters attack the continents, gnawing them, rending them, and finally dispersing them. The immense flowers on whose memory still float, like Brahminical gods, the shades of Pericles, of Virgil, of Dante, and of Raphael, are faded, after having scented the air with their perfumes; they have disappeared in the dissolution of their elements; and yet, in the breast of the surrounding world, as in ourselves, there is maintained a continuous antithesis between what seems and what is, and that is why the death of everything, instead of being the end of that thing, is but the commencement of its appropriation to new states. It is an inevitable law. From it results the permanence of the intelligent essence in this world and the nature of the rôle that this essence has come to play; it is by virtue of this law that what appears is linked to what was, and that the present at once comprises appreciable portions of the past and of the future. Let us transport ourselves in imagination to the close of that epoch that is called the Age of

Pericles. Euripides is dying; Phidias is
dead, his dearest pupils are dead; the great
period is definitively ended. Yet nothing
is destroyed; all the means save one—a
capital element, it is true—exist for the
production of new creations. Along with
the value, the savor, the perfume, the
particular stamp of the extinct period,
with the structure that was peculiar to it
and the special soul that animated it, has
disappeared forever what one may call the
masculine germ that is contained, and
which conferred upon it the individuality
of its being; this germ is dissolved, it
counts no more in the total of the world's
wealth, it will never appear again. But
behind it remains the floating mass of
what may be called feminine elements,
endowed with a receptivity calculated to
result in new creations when a new
plastic cause, furnished by a new race,
shall have reawakened the paralysed
fecundity.

Thus from the Greek detritus, held sus-

pended in the depths of men's minds and
touched by Roman intelligence, emerges
the Age of Augustus. Into the womb of
this enervated profusion of antique Hel-
lenic beauty, the savage freshness of Italic
sentiment introduces chemical combina-
tions, and one sees arise under forms,
and with tendencies, hitherto unknown,
the Aeneid, the Odes, the book of Lucretius, the comedies of Plautus, the elegies
of Catullus, and the temples and rich
buildings that are scattered over the
flanks of the Palatine.

Was this better? Was this equal to
those regretted splendors? It was different. Here was perfect beauty no longer,
but the domination of solidity and magnificence. A singular impression of force
made itself felt. A tendency of ideas, a
correctness of thought, a breadth of doctrine, a disposition to generalise the conception of beauty; something more human,
but rigid, hard, firm, despotic, prosaic,
taught the generations of that age both

reality and precision. Men no longer felt that childish joy in living, that gaiety which is content with action, seeking nothing behind what glitters; the happy cult of existence crowned with the first roses had passed; unrecoverable, lost forever was something divine, celestial, Olympian, which of old time had moistened with its nectar the smiling lips of Anacreon and Alcaeus. Thenceforward the haughty command of Rome resounded upon the hardened ear; the troubled air was vibrant with the sound; a rigorous correctness sought to encompass all within a net of bronze.

And yet this world believed itself an imitation of the Greeks. It was mistaken, but it thrust upward, grew in its turn and arose, superb flower, as of old that other flower had lifted itself above the surface of the centuries. It was gnawed at as that other flower had been by the irreconcilable enemies of duration; it drooped, and, quitting the immortal atoms of which it was composed, it lost its soul and remained in dissolution until the day when Germanic fecundation gave life to a new blossom.

Just as the Romans had believed that they were Greeks, so the lettered monks, the learned bishops, the professors of Paris, Cologne and Padua, the architects and sculptors of Corbie, Strasburg, and Assisi, took themselves for Romans. The Alsatian Benedictin, Gunther, in writing his *Ligurinus* for Frederick II of Swabia, considered himself Vergilian! He and his contemporaries were far from that. What the delicate folk of Rome had called beauty would have been understood by no one in that age.

On the other hand, men had never contemplated a vaster accumulation of ideas. The mind in search of facts unrelated to ancient times lacked the power to express with elegance, or even clarity, what it drew from itself and what it gathered elsewhere: it was too active, too hurried; it desired too much; it gave, took, de-

manded; it never rested; suddenly and at
once it aspired to too many conquests,
and lost itself in the pursuit of innumerable
dreams that had issued from every cranny
of the most prodigious imagination ever
known. Antiquity, Roman avidity, had
been content to pursue their fates within
a rather narrow geographic circle. The
Middle Age aspired to know the entire
globe, as well as to explore the nature of
the soul and of God in their most hidden
secrets. Saturated with Burgundian,
Gothic, Frankish, Norman and Lombard
blood, its veins were throbbing with
covetousness, ambition and activity in all
their forms. It was on the move, it was
coming and going, it was traveling, search-
ing, listening, it was expressing, and it was
flung to the very antipodes of the majestic
placidity of the Greek world, and as far
again from the haughty security of the
Cæsars. I have said that this age believed
itself Roman; I repeat; it believed itself
Roman! In imagination it was filled with

inspirations of the Latin muse, giving as proof of this its persistent attachment to the ancient language. It plumed itself also upon being the pupil of Byzantine decadence; while the scholars, artists, writers and politicians of Byzantium declared themselves Greeks, because for their part they reproduced many subjects dealt with by Alexandrian carvers; but without realizing it, and too absorbed in their ideas to be aware of their impotence to imitate, they presented the charming subjects under the dry, anatomical forms in which the austere images of their saints were arrayed.

The Middle Age was a great inventor. In politics it conceived of the personal right, and established it in the face of the sovereign's prerogatives. It held this right inviolable and denied, in principle, that the safety of the State is the measure of its subjects' security. In the arts, less thoughtful of the ensemble than of detail, it sought a refined ideal; on marble, stone, and the parchment of missels, it wished to imprint facial expressions with a precision, with a kind of exaltation of reality, of which neither Greece nor Rome had ever felt the slightest need. What it achieved is so marvelous, so finished, that many a cathedral statue may be placed as high as any creation of antique art in its most perfect development.

What made this epoch, above all, was the diffusion throughout all Europe of an equal passion for seeing, creating, penetrating, and transfiguring things in accordance with a mode superior to earthly conditions. This was not the preoccupation of one man, of one school, of a single city, of a small area; it took possession of a continent. Men sometimes adventured on different ways, but they were in search of the same things. In politics, for example, the guilds and the Hanseatic League were unlike the communes of Flanders, and the cities of Provence and Languedoc; but everywhere men longed equally for rights, franchises, and the means of liberty;

and so eager was everyone to accentuate his individuality, that men everywhere wished for privileges, to boot,—a notion absolutely foreign to the antique world— and, in fact, privileges existed everywhere for everyone, even for the lepers. In architecture, individual styles distinguished themselves because originality was overflowing: an Italian cathedral borrowed scarcely anything from its sister across the Rhine; but the same stamp was none the less impressed on all varieties, because nowhere did men remain strangers to the passion for the infinite. As for literature, armed, helmeted, lance in rest, impregnated with the spirit of adventure, it paraded the heroes of its chivalric poems from Constantinople to Iceland, with their mad bravado, their passion for independence, their need of action and the unrestrained temperament that made these characters the incarnation of all then thought most brilliant, most eloquent and most intrepid.

Another peculiar feature of this flowering of the Middle Age is that no period absorbed so great a portion of its power that one may state that such and such a date was the moment of moments, that then bloomed the flower *par excellence*. In the case of the Greeks, such an observation is possible: they enjoyed sixty incomparable years. It is possible, too, in the case of the Romans; the great light burned for a century and a little more. But the Middle Age took up its work at the very beginning, and thenceforward, stronger here, weaker there, it never ceased until the end to act, to busy itself with everything, to interrogate, to doubt, to desire and not to desire.

For this there were two reasons. The active, masculine Germanic element was everywhere; here more abundant, there less so; allied, balanced and shaped in different ways, but in reality always the same. Then, too, religion furnished the different centers of activity with identical maxims and habits. In full view of every intellectual work-shop—at Burgos as at Hambourg, in London and Dublin as in Venice and Florence—there arose the same general outline and an absolute identity of potential subjects. What was individual in this series of pictures, was the colors: in the south and in the north objects appear under very different lights.

This vital movement attained its culminating point in the twelfth and thirteenth centuries. Thereafter it declined until the fourteenth. Then there manifested itself with increasing definiteness the transforming cause that existed in the heart of that society. This cause was intimately bound up with the state of religion.

Such is the nature of the souls of the elect that they consider the good which unites the Creator to his creatures only at that elevated point where it is neither touched nor blighted by human hands. Souls of this quality are little concerned

with observing whether or not the divine
feet of the celestial verities, resting upon
earth, are spotted with a little mud; they
are not disturbed as to this; they look only
upon the faces of the immortal travelers,
and, with glance fixed upon their brows,
they compass them about with all their
thoughts, with all their affections, across
the immaculate spaces through which they
are led by them. This is admirable, no
doubt, but so noble an absorption in the
infinite is never the lot of the majority:
the bulk of mankind is less interested in
transcendental sublimity than in what
falls beneath the blunt perception of its
senses.

Religion had commenced by giving
pliancy to the Germanic spirit and furnish-
ing it with reasons for sociability. It had
given it a model of organization in proffer-
ing the forms of the Holy Empire; in the
canonical law it had presented it with a
legislation recognised by all the conquered;
by insisting upon the patronage of the

bishops, defenders of their cities, it had saved the middle classes, if not from all illegal attempts, at least from the legality of serfdom; it had preserved in its convents, and multiplied under monkish pens, copies of the classic works along with the folios of its theology; it had built the cities of Germany and of Switzerland, of a part of England, of a part of France, of a part of Spain, and even in Italy it had founded or restored more than one city wall. The most flourishing villages rose up about its monasteries, and just as surely as the eleventh century would have had no schools—still less the universities then flourishing in all Christian kingdoms—without the intervention of the Church, so certainly would there have been no agriculture, no clearing of the land, without the monks; no marshes would have been drained, no regions made healthful; and the mills, the forges, and most necessary factories would never have been established. The monks were active because they were disciplined, and they alone, in the Western world, were disciplined at this time. Active, they became rich and held at their command more resources than feudal lords and kings; they alone could accomplish that great work, the creation of modern Europe.

Therefore it was just and right that the thankfulness of the people should surround the altars; they could not do less. Everyone realized the nature of his debt to the Catholic organization; and the common consciousness of this was so deeply rooted that when the day arrived that study and controversy resulted in heresy showing its head in the very heart of these most useful convents, public sentiment grew wroth and stamped out the innovators. Everyone took part in the suppression: kings, nobles, bourgeois, peasants. Such was the experience of Roscelin de Compiègne, Abelard, Wyclif, the Albigenses, the Pastoureaux, and so many others. The contemners of the Church were gainsaying the conviction and the interests of their time.

Thus the ecclesiastical hierarchy, being so well protected, found itself placed above all peril. And it rejoiced in its security. None the less, its blessings had borne their fruits, the times were slowly changing; no longer did the laity let the actions of the monks pass without criticism. They had learned what it was their business to know; now they wished to charge themselves with the pursuit of their own interests. The peasants united under the protection of the abbeys and the chateaux, instructed and guided by the ones, guarded by the others, had grown rich in rural labor; they had become powerful enough to meditate *jacqueries*. There is no reason to misunderstand this matter; history furnishes proofs regarding it on every occasion. The peasant who is really miserable, maltreated and downtrodden, never revolts. If oppression goes too far, he takes flight; he lives in woods and caves,

and if he possesses arms he uses them
against wild beasts; but the hereditary
cowardly and crafty temperament of the
man of the soil forbids him to lift his head
save under the influence of covetousness
and envy. He has never fought for liberty.
The peasants of the twelfth, thirteenth and
fourteenth centuries, under one form or
another, here more and there less, began
to feel the prick of will-power, at the same
time that they saw themselves treated
with greater consideration. In England
the yeoman had become a power, a re-
spected part of the common strength. He
furnished the camps with those redoubtable archers who played so great a rôle in
the wars of the Edwards. The Spanish
peasants, accustomed to fight against the
Moors, as though they had been knights,
scarcely held themselves at a less price;
the rural communes of southern France,
under the leadership of their *souldics*,
proved themselves as proud as the vil-
lagers of the Apennines and the Romagna.

The rustic of central and northern France was less comfortable; nor were the agricultural multitudes of Germany, Slavs subject to German overlords, lifting their heads very high. In these regions too, however, labor had borne its fruits; men possessed, and clung to their possessions; they had learned much from the monks; and they were beginning to look around them.

The bourgeoisie was going further. Whatever may have been said on the subject, the fact is that the bourgeoisie never lost its franchises even in the darkest and most difficult moments of the general transformation. It suffered, but who did not suffer? It suffered, but it lived; and there came a day when its knowledge reached as far as the monks'; it was capable of guiding itself while taking counsel only of its own wisdom. Whereupon it let the advice of its preceptors fall upon deaf ears; it developed into a class that was opulent, arrogant, opinionated, ambitious, turbulent, rapacious, intelligent, and capable of as much good as evil; it populated and swelled London and Edinburgh, Saragossa, and Valladolid, the imperial cities of Germany and Switzerland, the good towns of France, and the communes and republics of Genoa, Florence, Milan, Venice, Pisa and Sienna, to count only the most notable of the innumerable centers of population that then overspread all Europe. The citizens of that day reached a point at which they felt themselves no longer bound to the monks in any way. They cultivated the land without them; they manufactured their woolens and their silks without them; they governed without them, and the companions and master workmen of Flanders asked no priest to expound the theory of insubordination. Nevertheless, the age (bourgeois, peasants, nobles) remained Catholic; no one dreamed of emancipating the mind from what had been believed and hoped until then. But ideas of a really offensive nature were

already germinating. The ancient paganism had left behind it more numerous and
deeper traces than men suspected; the
crusades had awakened the imagination in
many ways, and commerce with the
Levantine countries was slowly and obscurely effecting the transportation of
strongly heterodox notions and moral
tendencies. The dissident dogmas that
had been so terribly suppressed at their
first appearance had never been abrogated;
they still circulated as items of no import.
Such a condition does not enfeeble certain
ideas. The barons were quick to resist
the clergy and even to despoil them; everyone, from the least and meanest serf to
the proudest monarch, was apt at mock-
ing vices as weaknesses of the clerical order.
They came to take a peculiar pleasure in
the accusatory songs, in the caricatures
done by sculptors and painters. Dante
publicly plunged the Popes into the out-
rageous flames of Hell.

There was reason for this. If the faith

of Christ could never suffer the least de-
preciation, the human army of the Church
had submitted to the law of mortal things;
the worm of corruption had found lodging
in the over fattened flesh. The clerks,
long considered the best of counselors and
the surest guides, never being contradicted by anyone, had ceased to give sage
advice, still less did they furnish profitable
examples; freely they indulged in what
was most reprehensible. If the minstrels
and the jongleurs of France, if the master
singers of the Hanseatic cities reproached
them with slothfulness, impiety, debauch-
ery in all its forms, simony, and the complete forgetfulness of their simplest duties,
it was but plain truth. The day was to
come when Michael Angelo, an essentially
pious man, could cry: "A monk in a picture! How could the work help being
spoiled, since the monks have spoiled the
world?" What Michael Angelo said in the
sixteenth century had already become
universally thought in the fourteenth,

and so it was that society in the Middle
Age found itself in the singular position
of believing and scorning, of accepting
and repulsing, of upholding and dis-
honoring.

But a society may long survive such
gnawing pains. What happened in Europe
at this time is the proof of it. Men re-
spected by habit, they denigrated by evidence. In reality society did not know
what side to take; what it possessed seemed
blighted, but it had nothing to put in its
place. For this dual cause, all went
haltingly. With Boccaccio, men said to
themselves: If religion continues to exist,
despite the manners of sovereign pontiffs,
cardinals, bishops and monks, it is obvious
that it is divine.

For a long time men cherished this
paradox, which scarcely served to tran-
quilize their consciences. Little by little,
however, the nations who had grown
weary of having the extravagances of the
clergy under their eyes, found sustenance

in a kind of practical atheism, seasoned
with nauseous superstitions. It may be
stated as a fact that the fifteenth century
no longer believed in anything, that it
no longer admitted anything, and that it
was only because of weariness, prudence
and ignorance that it did not change anything.

But at last there arose in various quar-
ters doctors who grew wroth and de-
nounced the evil. Nor did they scruple to
reveal its depths and its perils. The
chancellor of the University of Paris,
Gerson, a person whose orthodoxy and
whose virtue remained above all suspicion,
uttered the severest strictures; and he was
not alone. Men demanded that the
scandal end; they stigmatized the morbid
torpor in which the clergy slumbered;
they said that if a prompt and radical
remedy were not applied to these carnal
insurrections, the Church of God was
exposed to death. At this very moment
a schism crowned the work; two Popes,

two colleges of cardinals, who refused to
relinquish their dynasties, gave justice
to all reproaches. Then the cup over-
flowed and flagrant heresies appeared upon
the scene: Jerome of Prague and John
Huss had raised the standard of the chalice.

If ever a man attacked by a chronic
malady could succeed in curing himself by
simply recognizing his danger, few patients
would succumb. Corporations would enjoy the same advantage. But it never falls
out thus. Once introduced by the tooth
of secular corruption, the poison courses in
the veins; evidence regarding it, the certain knowledge of its consequences do
not furnish the means for its suppression.
The number of wise men always remains
infinitely less than that of the fools: the
minds that are turned toward good are
units, while those who dwell in evil, as the
salamander in the fire, are legion; and so
the fact runs on to its consequences. What
becomes of the excellent and incontestable
advice that is proffered? Mere common

place: it is proclaimed by the people least disposed to apply it, and the bad is peacefully followed by the worst. To escape from its difficulties, the fifteenth century convened the council of Constance. Complaints were so general, so powerful, and so well founded that it was necessary to give evidence of a desire for better things; but nothing came of it. They burned two heretics, they applied expedients; but at bottom things remained what they had become.

Thenceforward, with the despair of changing anything, indifference grew, and from this was born the idea of dispensing with religious probity. Men became the more tranquil regarding the future of the Church as the world seemed to concern itself less and less with problems of morality and dogma. Why revolt against something in which one was not interested? The mass of the clergy, the bishops who never visited their dioceses, the canons who never appeared at their chapters, the

curates who did not reside in their parishes,
the abbots who let their monasteries fall
to ruin while they converted their manses
into elegant mansions, the monks who
spent in taverns and elsewhere all the time
that the carelessness of their superiors
allowed them; in fine the clergy, in its
entirety, exceptions aside, abandoning
themselves in the byways, came more and
more to be no clergy at all. Conventual
and secular vows seemed never to have
existed. That was a trifle; the most
essential rules of conduct and good sense
were equally forgotten. The pastors of
souls no longer addressed themselves to
their flocks; they did not know what
religious teaching was; spiders toiled on
the altars; and have not I, who write these
lines, seen in the register of master Cor-
feuilhe, notary of Bordeaux, under the
date of June 17, 1568, a protest signed by
my eighth grandfather, Etienne, against
the beneficed priests of his parish of
Sainte-Colombe who, on the very day of

Corpus Christi, absented themselves with
the result that the faithful were forced
to seek out the fathers of Saint Augustine
in order to hold service? And Etienne was
not a malevolent man, but on the contrary a zealot who turned his hand to the
work of Saint-Bartholomew.

As the clergy was no longer performing
its function, to what did it turn its activity?
To seizing the revenue of benefices, to
augmenting it by pretensions, by demands,
by institutions, by contrivances, with the
result that the entire Christian religion,
its mysteries, its dogmas, its morality, its
teaching, its mysticism, and the scholarly
energies of its immense and splendid
establishment, tended to become nothing
more than the various wheels of a fiscal
machine that worked for the profit of a
single class whose founders had, in truth,
created Europe, but whose representatives
thenceforward were to serve primarily to
pervert it.

And then those non-Christian elements,

recently noted, commenced to assume importance, condensing themselves under pressure of a fact which held a considerable place in the attention of the people at the beginning of the fourteenth century.

The feudal world sincerely considered itself as being nothing more than the continuation, pure and simple, of what had preceded it. As it conceived things, Themistocles and Pompey had been only barons; it found no difficulty in numbering Alexander and Cæsar in the company of valiant knights. It dressed the men of past times in its own fashion. Few minds were exempt from this error, Petrarch for example; but those who were slowly made disciples who in turn produced others, and the day finally came when by dint of constantly reading Vergil, Horace, Lucian, Cicero, Livy—reading them badly, but still reading them—men came to understand them otherwise than by the past. Whereupon they were astonished, intoxicated, exalted by their discovery; they perceived things of which they had never dreamed. Europe ceased to discover its spirit in what it read; its image was no longer reflected in what it contemplated. It found that it was disgusted with scholasticism, both because it had carried it to excess, and because scholasticism had said its last word and could no longer do more than repeat itself. Europe desired that Plato, and even Aristotle, should speak to it otherwise than they had previously done. In short, all men who thought a little and who reflected well or ill, began to enter upon a singular preoccupation, whose result was to communicate to ancient books so strong and so attractive a savor that the number of persons desiring education grew immeasurably; and, in the same proportion that enthusiasm increased, disgust, boredom, contempt, and indignation with the clergy took shape. Men thought that they were already in possession of an order of ideas capable of replacing the order they had so long traduced.

This, however, was an error. They were masters of nothing at all, or, rather, the diversity of viewpoints opened by their studies was such that anarchy of opinion was immeasurably augmented. Everyone, in Spain, in Germany, in Flanders, in France, in Italy, saw things after his own fashion, preferring one book to another and this opinion to that. Some had drawn the most audacious materialism from Lucretius' apóstrophe to Nature; some were seeking in Phædon an ethereal spiritualism, and were refining on Christian purity along this line; but many, made quite giddy by the heady enthusiasm into which rediscovered antiquity had plunged them, were allowing themselves to glide smilingly towards the most brutal paganism, because they gave ear to the harmonious language of Horace, seeing him as beautiful as antique love and, like it, crowned with roses. The myriad ideas which were in agitation, which, now awakened, flew from all sides, resembled swarms of bees that had been excited in their hives by the first light, the newborn freshness and the perfumes of the dawn. Coming forth in a mass, animated, curious, eager, agitated, turbulent, and buzzing, they flung themselves upon all flowers, sipping at every plant and moving in all directions, they risked themselves on all heights, while abandoning themselves to the puffs of every breeze.

Never had more ardent curiosity stirred the human mind, nor had at its disposition such diverse means of action and such powerful talents. The inhabitant of Germany brought to this work his power of reflection, his tenacity, his tendency to mystic revery, and his inexhaustible thirst for detail; the Englishman his violence of resolution; the Fleming his disposition to let nothing deceive him: the Frenchman furnished little; he had already acquired the habit of administrative ré-

gime, and the military spirit cultivated
in him nothing but soldierly vanity. As
for the Spaniards, victors over Moorish
courage, infatuated by their triumphs,
the astonished conquerors of an unhoped
for world whose riches seemed incalculable,
they, considering themselves masters
everywhere, set no limits whatsoever to
the intrepidity of their pride, and they
were as dangerous in religion as in politics.
All these hosts were briskly advancing
to overturn the ancient order.

Beyond all doubt, the men of that day,
wandering far from the slopes of the past,
were dominated by their violent curiosity.
That was the chief sentiment. They
seemed to awaken from a sleep broken
by dreams that had never showed them
the realities. In relation to the Greeks,
the Romans had never been the astonished disciples that the men of the Middle
Age were in relation to the Romans. It
seemed in this latter epoch that the great
interest, the great end of existence was

primarily to read and to admire lost works. No one believed himself possessed of an original sentiment, and had one been so it would have been no cause for glorification; quite the contrary, such a notion would have been held as a link binding one to the time from which one affected to escape. Theirs was the positiveness of youth. If the destiny that conducts men were not always wiser than men's aims, this period of seething activity would never have created the magnificence that issued from it; it would have produced nothing but pure pedantry and pedants, the flood of which, at the outset, was beyond all calculation.

What is most clearly evident is that men wished to escape from the ways in which they had been walking, and that each turned his face to a star that was shining in some other direction; but while the greatest number of innovators were seeking outside the Christian faith, more or less afield, a path that would lead to an unknown flowering, a nucleus of minds, more conscious of the true conditions of human development, continued to subsist, and this group was never willing for a moment to bow to the pretensions of Platonists, Stoics, Peripatetics, Eleatics, or Sceptics: it continued to remain faithful to tradition, starting from the doctrines of its ancestors, from the essential element of social life, while it rescued from mud and stones, the mired, befouled, and half-rotted car of the Church.

In the fifteenth century, as in all climacteric epochs, the adversaries of the present ranged themselves under three standards. Some, the most ardent, crudely stamped as infamous everything that had been produced since the twelve Cæsars. To them the world appeared shamefully abused and degraded; boldly they turned back their sleeves to destroy what displeased them; they constituted themselves executioners. They accomplished nothing. Radicalism of whatever sort can never find a footing in the world. The ferocious adversaries which clerical deportment had raised up against Christianity frankly wished to destroy it, and so little did they succeed that there was no need even of repressing them. Their madness was only an impotent dilettantism.

At the side of these ardent revolutionists appeared men who were desirous of finding a mean between pagan antiquity and what had succeeded it. These men turned their glances toward the primitive Church. With the two testaments in their hands, and the writings of the fathers beneath their eyes, they presumed to restore the dogma to its primitive simplicity and to extirpate the interpolated corruptions. No one realized that it is no more possible to check the growth of an institution than it is to halt an organic being, and that every living thing issues from infancy to undergo successively the other phases of existence. If one is dissatisfied with the moral proclivities or with the

physical structure of an adult creature, it
is absurd to seek a process capable of
reducing it to some anterior moment of
its life when it was more pleasing. Yet
it was this dream which preoccupied the
judgment of a great number of well-
intentioned persons at the close of the
fifteenth century. In vain the Bohemian
heretics had been put to death; their
investigative inclinations persisted, and
men were more than ever determined to
rediscover in the dogma what was primitive, to disengage it, and to oppose it to
what they supposed could be amputated
at will without the subject necessarily
dying. The mind which pursued this
dangerous study was naturally ill disposed
toward the ecclesiastical hierarchy, which
it judged neither legitimate nor useful.

This extra-Catholic disposition was observed with a just terror by certain other
pious and upright persons who, firmly
attached to the Church, would have liked
to purify it without imposing on it any

essential change. These good servitors
wished neither subversions nor mutila-
tions; more or less bold, more or less
sagacious, they realized that the clergy
could not, however, remain what it was.
Unhappily the efforts of this group, which
was the most worthy of interest because
it was the most sagacious, lacked energy,
as is most often the case with right think-
ing, the unpopular privilege of minorities.
A system of moderation never acquires
the support of interested passions, either
of the attack, or of the defence. But while
it was being prophesied on all sides that
religious changes would furnish the principal characteristic of the century, the
human spirit, following its destiny regard-
less of the previsions of men, was demon-
strating quite another thing.

The ages of the world, like individuals,
have but slight perception of what con-
stitutes their chief originality. The fifteenth century failed to discern one feature
of its physiognomy, which was very small

no doubt and indistinct, but which,
growing rapidly, was destined to become
its particularly glorious mark. Men aspired to knowledge, and they succeeded in
seizing it; they sought to unite the elements
of an armed theology at war with the
Church; on the other hand, they wished
to bring the clergy back to a realization
of its duties, to a realization of its dangers;
in politics, power sought to consolidate
itself, to extend itself and a generally felt
need of security came to its aid, despite
the no less general taste for turbulent
liberties. While admitting that success
crowned some of these proclivities to the
detriment of others, men had acquired
nothing very new; a few more rights, a
little more truth, a little more good sense,
a little more calm; but all these for a time
more or less short, since nothing endures.
However, the fifteenth century had received from its predecessors a preoccupation of rarer merit, on which I have already
touched in passing.

As Greece understood the representation
of the human being, beauty was the supreme end and to attain it the rest was
sacrificed. This was the system of the
great schools, this the motive of their
high perfection. The idealization of the
body, the complete balance of its separate
parts, certain refinements which nature
gives scarcely, if at all—such as the sim-
plification of the planes of the thorax, a
slightly accentuated smallness of the head,
and, in the models nearest archaism, an
almost excessive paecision of certain mus.
cles—these had been the study of antiquity
at its best. Later the Alexandrian epoch
set out in search of grace; it found it and
did not escape mannerism, but no more
than the preceding schools did it attach
capital importance to the moral expression
of its subjects. If it sometimes encountered it under the chisel, it was exception-
ally, fugitively; it did not make a system
of it. Perhaps the Niobe evokes the idea
of sorrow, it does not display it; again one

may admit that the Laocoon carries on face and limbs a reflection of the soul, one may also question it; but in any case the principal value of this group lies in the observation of certain rules, the harmony of proportion and the nobility of attitude.

The Romans were not afraid to reproduce ugliness, for they were in quest of reality. They liked to depict negroes and even persons who were deformed or disfigured. Their temperament relished the trivial; they were coarse, they took a great pleasure in caricatures, and their disposition to recoil at no deviation from the rules of beauty led them to the conclusion that when an emperor was ugly it was necessary to represent him as he was, nor did they fail to do so.

It was this side of art that saved the rest in the epoch of decadence. The Byzantines became the morose and exact interpreters of those Church fathers who wished to represent Our Lord as a repulsive type, who praised the virgins of vulgar aspect

and the hideous saints, to the end that no
concession might be made to sensuality;
they invented emaciation, fleshless faces
and bodies, ossified limbs, and on the
consular diptychum of the fourth and
fifth centuries they found precisely the
anatomical models that they required.
This fashion continued for many long
years. But toward the twelfth century a
transformation made itself apparent. It
occurred to men to express as exactly as
possible the sentiments of characters by
choice of attitudes and facial expressions.
It was a revolution. An innovation unknown to Greeks and Romans appeared in
the world.

The artists of Low Saxony and of
Flanders, the artists of France and Italy,
discovered the secret. They ceased to
hold with the Byzantines that dry, cold,
dead ugliness was a divine institution;
they conceived the idea of rendering com-
prehensible to the spectator the holy joy
of the Virgin contemplating the divine

Infant; the respectful exultation of Saint
Joseph watching the play of the Saviour;
the prodigious meditation of Saint John
writing at Patmos; and especially and constantly, with refinements more and more
delicate, the youthful, virginal, wholly
pure, wholly celestial countenance of the
Queen of the Angels. These artists followed the Roman tradition in the sense
that they never recoiled from the repro-
duction of common and even repulsive
faces, again they remained faithful to
Byzantine lessons, for they preserved in
general the consecrated attitudes and
vestments: but they studied with a care
never before exercised the plastic resources
of human physiognomy; it was not
grand and simple expressions that they
sought most, but rather complex expressions, tenderness, ecstasy, restrained joy,
stifled sorrow. The image makers—they
must be accorded this glory—pushed this
system to perfection; but when they had
reached the highest point, which was about

the middle of the fifteenth century, it was discovered that heads so animated, so speaking, so alive, could no longer be superimposed on fantastic and artificial bodies, and that it was absolutely necessary, moreover, to place these finished types in the midst of a setting worthy of them. Consequently men were enthralled in the study of what? Of the Beautiful; and the great inspiration of that age, Antiquity, presented itself to the artists and imposed on them its lessons. Antiquity, which was already turning the heads of politicians, theologians, scholars, philosophers, and poets, became still more definitely the sovereign of sculptors and of painters. It revealed to them God's creatures and God himself, trees and tombs, earth and grass, the wide horizon and the fleecy sea, and the deep azure of the Empyrean, as they had never seen or dreamed of all these things. The great originality, the great instrument of glory that the new age was carrying in its breast, then became manifest: it was the gift of plastically rendering the human soul, the soul of nature, and of representing to the eye and mind all this wealth that was yet untouched. This is enough that the world should be forever constrained to proclaim with unanimous voice that never on the blue waters of time has there opened a flower whose golden petals, whose sumptuous foliage, may be praised above the miraculous flowering of the fifteenth century. I shall not go to the length of saying that there has never been anything equal to this; it would not be true: but the epoch that is called the Renaissance is inferior to no other whatsoever.

At the dawn of the movement with which we are concerned, toward the middle of that solemn fifteenth century, the eyes of all nations were turned toward Italy, and for this reason one concludes that Italy outshone the rest of the world. It was instinctive. Eyes sought brilliancy, and brilliant Italy attracted them. In that country was opening the most abundant source of the civilization that was destined to overflow the world.

Assuredly one might have found elsewhere certain very important tendencies that this land could not display at all, or which it possessed in a very inferior degree, tendencies which were later to play their rôle: but at this given moment Italy answered to all calls. Of old, like the rest of Europe, it had experienced the happy effects and the lamentable shocks resulting from the dissolution of the ancient world and the new mastery of the northerners. The latter had nobly modified the blood of those miserable colonists, those descendants of slaves and children of freedmen, with which the imperial administration had peopled Tuscany, Milan, Venetia, and Emilia. It was chiefly in the north and the center that this mixture had taken place, so it was natural that the principal vitality of Italy should preferably manifest itself in this region. Men had evidence of it when the time came. Then the peninsular merchant, part Burgundian, Goth, Langobard, and Roman, marched proudly against the feudal lord, and he too, with his sword at side and shield on shoulder, styled himself free, a sovereign and a tyrant, and proved the truth of his words. What came forth from this very brief conflict, terminated by the victory of the industrial class, were not bourgeoisies in the sense that we understand them, but many patrician states; and it was in vain that Venice, Genoa, Florence, Sienna, Lucca, Alexandria, Pisa, all the cities, all the towns, and even all the villages, took unto themselves the title democratic, and proclaimed the rights and victories of the *Popolani* over the *Nobili*. The *populus romanus* was still alive in their imaginations, but not the *plebs*. If one renounced one's arms, when one became citizen after being gentleman, it was to take others. One built oneself a palace, one dressed in fine cloth, velvets and silk, and one trailed at one's heels the same band of armed servants that one had formerly commanded. In addition, a proud inequality was carefully maintained between the various trades: those who made damask would not shake the hands of those who dealt in wool. Men wore armor, went mounted, made war, and ruled the State.

They went too far. Government became impossible. Venice alone knew how to manage and, having thrust the immense majority of its inhabitants into a subordinate rank by a most necessary and excellent *coup d'état*, it had the honor to found the most legitimate of powers, by the simple act of assuring its people glory and repose, and it outlasted all the State constitutions ever known. Everywhere else a feverish condition was established, whose repeated paroxysms put the life of the patient in danger at every moment. This patient could be sustained only by expedients, and what expedients?

Just as medicine has recourse in certain cases to the use of poisonous substances, so the Italian States existed by murderous methods. Impotent to found anything that was stable, they sought resource in instability: the magistrates were temporary, and very temporary; during their period of office they were throttled by the rival authority of many councils; but as the Italians considered it dangerous, even then, to put themselves under the rule of a compatriot, they invented the idea of calling in a foreigner, in order that he should have no influence, enjoy no respect, and not imagine that he had a future. But despite such rigorous precautions, one saw everywhere nothing but usurped power, tyrannies that were open or suspected, and hence cruel and bloody; the traces of poignard and of poison were constantly evident in political schemes, and interminable bands of exiles wandered from one city to another, awaiting the day when they, in turn, could expel those of their execrated rivals whom they did not butcher.

One pictures to oneself the habits of these citizens who were ceaselessly harassed by skilled murder, to be feared or to be committed. In the narrow, dark, and tortuous streets, the house doors were low so that they should be difficult to enter and easy to defend. The walls were spaced with loop holes, so that one might fire from shelter upon the detested neighbor, with arrow or cross-bow arrow, and later with arquebuse. If one had to stir abroad at moments when quarrels were most flagrant, one was not so mad as to walk in the center of the way; one slipped along the walls, and while walking one's eyes were alert and one's hand near one's dagger. Even at home, with closed doors, with wife and children, one remained on guard; one tested what one ate and drank; above all one did not lie down to bed without having visited the lodge and meticulously barred the doors.

Spirits were hardy, and temperaments singularly passionate. Just as one strove to become master of his city and stab the members of the opposing party, so one loved to frenzy and was jealous with surpassing rage. Florentine precautions were immoderate. Women were confined in their homes more closely than in harems. Dante, recounting the stories of Pia and of Francesca da Rimini has shown how tender passages might end; while Boccaccio has revealed in his delightful language, presenting the imagination with the most charming landscapes and the most enchanting scenes, how they might succeed.

It seems that this singular country, so agitated, so tormented, so revolutionary, so cruel, so ferocious, and so criminal, must have been of somber humor. Not at all. It was as gay, as lively, as brilliant as it was sociable; by this it was distinguished from other countries more or less brutal, more or less surly. It knew all ambitions, and the most contrasting ones; it loved liberty with the same abandon that it sought despotism. When men were not engaged in butchery, they were embracing with the most vehement affection; and, after participating in conspiracies compact of the most unheard of perfidies, they sedulously constructed the most delicate sonnets. Literature soon became an important occupation; while the rest of Europe still esteemed only metaphysics, Italy placed elegance of speech in the first rank of mental accomplishments. Those rich merchants, those pitiless usurers who weighed gold and wrote their notes in the shops of Venice, Florence, and Perugia, those rapacious speculators who spread the nets of their avarice as far as London, as far as Antwerp, and who pushed their fleets beyond Holland, were exacting amateurs of poetry. And this was because the Latin muses had never quite ceased to live on the soil that of old time had given them birth.

Of collections of ancient manuscripts

there was no lack.   Here they were con-
sulted more often than in the north; here,
in all times, they had been better understood.   Hence it was that when minds
reawakened, Italy, if not the only country
to find its footing, accomplished the feat
more quickly and more solidly.   It took
the head of the procession that was turning
and climbing back toward antiquity.   In
Italy art had been especially familiar with
the Byzantine and Roman styles; it had
been ignorant of the different varieties of
Gothic; so it had remained always nearer
to the antique methods.   In this country,
too, a number of masterpieces had always
remained under the eyes of everyone.
From the thirteenth century onward, when
by chance they had drawn some statue
from the earth, they had sufficiently
esteemed it to place it safely in a sacristy.
The Italian mind could never understand
that a statue of Jupiter or of Venus was
unworthy the protection of a church.
When they began to reflect on beauty,

they attached a still greater value to
these treasures. Thenceforward they
wished to augment the number of antique
objects that had been found and exhumed
until then without anyone seeking them.
They had only to dig, and the tombs
opened before delighted eyes, masterpieces
were brought to life; and those glorious
dead, finding speech again, commenced
their lessons in the presence of an intoxicated crowd. But the taste for, and the
need of expression that was at once ideal,
true and living, existed in Italy as elsewhere; Germanic and Christian sentiment
was not content with ancient beauty: it
desired the new; like the Flemish taste,
it was fascinated by the facial revelations
of the soul, with the result that the Byzantines found that they had formed pupils
far superior to themselves. The schools
that developed Giotto, Orcagna and Mas-
saccio were previsions of the most complete
productions of the modern conception.
They could not have reconciled them-

selves to simply acquired conquests. So
they did not turn back to antique art.
This was the greatest of blessings, but not
the only one.

Italy saw that it was more opulent than
any other region. Its immense commerce
had, beyond doubt, accumulated great
wealth in its counting houses; but this,
perhaps, was not even half of its fortune.
The fiscal constitution of Catholicism
brought to Rome abundant contributions
from the different States. These tributes
which, under a thousand forms, were
incessantly absorbed by the pontifical
chancellory, created resources that enabled
the leisurely great to encourage the culture
of the arts as well as the propagation of
vice. The Roman court spent its wealth
most freely on cooks, poisoners, perfumers,
dancers and bravoes; it gave little support
to men of letters; it had neither painters,
nor sculptors, nor architects, nor carvers,
nor goldsmiths before the reign of Julius
II. But as it did not keep tight hold upon

its money, it went into the rest of the
peninsula to encourage what was gaining
men's affection at that time. The magnificent Lorenzo de' Medici, and with him
the sovereigns of Ferrara, Mantua and
Urbino, furnished examples of an immoderate passion for the cult of intelligence. The
Bentivoglios, lords of Bologna, and the Pico
della Mirandolas closely followed such examples, and there was no feudatory so small
in the Romagna, no despot so inconsidera-
ble in the Republics, that he did not make
it a point of honor to sacrifice to the Muses.

Italy was scarcely Christian, and had
never been really so. In its imagination,
the Virgin had early assumed the attitude
of a Goddess; the saints had been trans-
formed into local Genii. Ecclesiastical
scandals, wantonly displayed in the city of
Saint Peter, had inspired in the people no
respect for saintly things. However, there
as elsewhere, men felt, and sometimes
keenly, that the clergy was not hearkening
to its vocation, that the apostolic doctrines

were dishonored without reason or justice by odious practices, and that the world had gained something that the pontifical throne should illumine with virtues instead of surrounding with mephitic vapors. It was by only a slight margin that one of the heresies most familiar to strayed Christian minds failed to triumph in Tuscany, when the disciples of Saint Francis of Assisi, true Ebionites, true shepherds, had sought to found the religion of the poor. The danger was so great and the fear so keen, that the Holy See began by compounding with the innovators. Afterwards it disarmed them; but their theory persisted in the face of clerical opulence: they continued to believe that the successors of the Galilean fisherman were made for modesty, humility, and indigence; that an arrogant and pampered clergy was an insulting anomaly to the Cross, and that the community of the faithful could be gathered into the fold— the road to which they had only too evidently lost—only by pastors who went barefooted, dressed in drugget, and carried crooks of wood. That was what the Italians of the fifteenth century thought, when they thought of religion. But it must be repeated that they thought of it less than men did elsewhere: they were too busy, they loved pleasure too well, they experienced too many and too diverse ambitions, they lived too much in the world, and, especially, they desired above everything else and sought overmuch what was spectacular.

These then were the conditions in which the inhabitants of the peninsula were living; Alexander VI, Borgia, occupying the chair of Saint Peter; the Aragonese reigning at Naples; the Venetians quarreling with the Dukes Sforza of Milan; the French, summoned by Ludovico il Moro, preparing to enter the Piedmont provinces; the Florentines, under Piero de' Medici, awakening from the intoxication into which they had been plunged by the masterful and captious administration of Lorenzo the Magnificent; the remainder of the country being sharply divided between Republics and Seigniories, and the traveling bands of condottieri seeking the pay of the first bidder, when, in many northern cities, there became manifest a singular sympathy for a certain Dominican monk whose predictions were bringing crowds flocking to him.

This monk, who had seemed destined by birth and fortune for a brilliant career, had entered the order as the result of a vocation which was all the more powerful for the fact that it had been strongly combated. He was a learned man, meditative, and a dreamer; he was never seen to smile; his constitution was weak, and he was often stricken by bodily debility. If he rose up again and held himself erect, it was under the spur of his will. An ardent faith possessed him. A prophet dear to the people, he did not argue, he affirmed, he imposed; heaven had bestowed on him the gift of authority. Those who listened to him felt themselves carried away and in his hand.   This monk was named Girolamo Savonarola.

The physique of this hero, for he was a hero, was short and frail; his chest was a little sunken; his bearing seemed that of a body charged with a soul too heavy.   But the yellow, thin, elongated face was lighted by the fire of two deep, black eyes that burned under thick brows.   The fine, pale hands moved nervously, but not without nobility, to accompany and emphasize the penetrating words that came from thin and lightly colored lips; the high, bulging forehead, whiter than the face, betrayed the predominance of imagination and enthusiasm over cold reason. . . .   But why draw the portrait of this man?   Behold himself!   There he is . . . pacing through the garden of the convent of Bologna. . . .   The weight of meditation bows him . . . he is not alone . . . he speaks . . . and we shall hear what he says.

PART II

CESARE BORGIA

Cesare Borgia

THE idea of uplifting Italy by uplifting its morals had come to naught. Savonarola had wished, by purely Catholic means, without touching either the unity of the Church or the tradition of the Faith, to cicatrize the wounds that were too acute. Not until long after his time, and then by the counter-stroke of triumphant heresy and schism, could the projects of the reformer receive a kind of application. As yet Italy was not ready to profit by this exclusively Gallican contrivance. For the moment, when the murderous flames in which the Dominican perished had been extinguished, any notion of achieving unity, liberty and order by the power of virtue was abandoned as the maddest of chimeras. What remained in the Italians' imagination was simply the necessity of closing their country's territory to intruders, of excluding them from participation in the wealth, splendors, art and enjoyments of a land that its inhabitants considered sacred; and the need of putting an end to the partition of this land, either by creating a single sovereignty, or a restricted number of sovereignties, whose first virtue would be to establish a force that would appear redoubtable to foreigners and be unconquerable by their ambitions.

The Spaniards held the southern extremity of the peninsula. But malevolence attacked them with far less force than it did the other foreigners. In the first place, they had long been masters of the country. The Italians were used to seeing them there. Again, this country itself was scarcely considered Italian, or at least in an inferior degree. It was called "the Kingdom"; it was a fife of the Holy See; but since the fall of the Western Empire, the fate of these provinces had been

CESARE BORGIA

peculiar. Byzantines had reigned over
them; then Arabs, then the Germans of
Hohenstaufen following the Normans;
then, momentarily, the French; and when
the Aragonese had succeeded to these
much handled leavings, they had not been
considered spoliators; they had only taken
what belonged to the first occupant. Besides, the manners of the Neapolitans were
not those of other peoples. Feudalism was
still alive among them, but it was not
vigorous; the great lords, constantly in
rebellion, were no less constantly fleeing
before a few lances sent from Castile. It
was a country slightly esteemed by its
neighbors, still less by its masters, peopled
with brutal, savage peasants and citizens
who were avaricious and basely corrupt.
In it the arts were indifferently cultivated.
Literature outshone the rest, but without
exciting much sympathy, for it was inspired
chiefly by the panegyric strain. For
these various reasons, so long as the
Italians were busy with other intruders,

they bore but a feeble ill-will against the Spaniards.

The Germans were the most offensive, and yet they were not excessively detested. As they were subjects and representatives of the Holy Roman Empire, it was recognized that they had a kind of right to interfere in the affairs of the peninsula. The Ghibellines leaned on them. The Guelfs did not desire an absolute rupture with them. Again, commercial relations with the Hanseatic cities were constant; science was highly honored in both countries, and, although they followed very different systems, each was much occupied with the arts. What annoyed and repelled was the rudeness of the soldierly German. But in those days men knew how to bear such inconveniences.

Malevolence fastened itself particularly on the French. One did not justify their rights to trouble Italy. They themselves were sure that "the Kingdom" must be their vested property because they were heirs of the House of Anjou. But without counting that this pretension had its source in nothing more than a pontifical whim, and a notably ancient one at that, the exercise of it had been neither happy nor brilliant. On the other hand, during the reign of Louis XI, the Genoese were responsible for throwing themselves into the arms of France; and, in the time of Charles VIII, it was Duke Ludovico of Milan who had organized the Neapolitan expedition, and who had opposed the Pope as well as the Aragonese with this invader whom he was soon to abandon and precipitate into the brawl of Fornovo. The people of Florence, for their part, were accustomed to affect a certain liking for the French kings; they readily declared them the protectors of their rights, and throughout the deceit, perfidy and treachery of both parties—the ordinary course of politics—this kind of fiction was maintained. However, in the final analysis, the Florentines like the Genoese, the

Milanese like the Pope, would not consent
to let their foreign allies, be they French,
German or Spanish, assume more than a
subaltern rôle. These foreigners were
clubs: they used them to belabor one
another, and counted on burning them
after victory.

After the Neapolitan expedition, Ludovico il Moro could no longer employ French
intervention, for he had too villainously
betrayed it. So he was to remain its
adversary. But King Louis XII, suc-
cessor to young Charles VIII, bravely
adapted himself to such hostility. As
Duke of Orleans, and representative of the
rights of Valenta Visconti, he reclaimed
the duchy; he seized it with incomparable
facility, a characteristic feature of all
French conquests during these wars, and
Ludovico, badly served, defeated, and
made prisoner, went to die in the château
of Loches after a captivity of ten years.
During this time many things were happen-
ing in the world, seized by the fever of

activity that was to shake it during the
first half of this century. The Turks,
under the leadership of princes who were
powerfully energetic, of barbarous will,
and possessed of ideas whose grandeur
equaled their contempt for the Christian
faith, served by troops superior to any
that the western kingdoms could oppose to them, were making their strength
felt and inspiring an immense terror,
which however did not distract the Eu-
ropean princes from the more pressing
business of destroying one another. Crusades were constantly talked of in Rome,
in Venice, in Valladolid, in Paris, even in
London, and especially in Vienna. But
at bottom, everyone, however little he
might be initiated into the passions of the
time, knew just how chimerical or mislead-
ing these proposals were. Their only
possible effect was to justify the vast
collections of money organized by the
Franciscan monks, who were strongly
suspected of being scarcely trustworthy

depositaries; nevertheless, the people kept on giving, giving, because they were afraid of the Turk. The court of Rome gathered to itself such of these profits as were not lost en route.

Meantime the Spaniards were continuing their trans-Atlantic discoveries. These passionately excited curiosity and general interest, and Castilian glory was augmented by this universal emotion. Everything that arrived from foreign countries, whose singularities were exaggerated, was calculated to disturb imaginations already so awakened: men of new color and new aspect, green birds, monkeys; delicate and bizarre creations wrought of feathers that were tinted with the most unexpected colors and shades; and, above all, much gold, much silver, and precious stones. It was said that over yonder precious metals littered the earth. Minds that were bold and given to lack of logic were intoxicated by such tales. Expeditions were organized in every country; they set out from Eng-

land as from France; but, next to the
Spaniards, the Portuguese proved themselves the luckiest. In order to gain
wealth, to conquer and to rule, to set out in
quest of what had never been seen before,
the sailors of Lisbon unhesitatingly con-
signed themselves to the hazard of the
waves across uncalculated wastes of unknown seas. In the first year of the
century, Alvarez Cabral, en route for the
East Indies, had been flung by a tempest
against a long reach of coast that was
resplendent with verdure. It was Brazil
that presented itself to him. This excite-
ment, which made adventurers of the
hardy men of the Iberian peninsula, did
not however send them all into far off
regions; they found booty and romance
nearer home; those Valencians, the Borgias, whose present head was occupying the
chair of Saint Peter, treated Italy as their
compatriots had treated Hispaniola, and
Don Cesare Borgia, the son of Alexander,
formerly cardinal, now captain, stalked

through central Italy just as Cortez some years later was to march across Mexico.

He had acquired the friendship of Louis XII, after vainly seeking a point of support in the Aragonese. It would seem that the latter, experts in ambition and rapacity, had trembled before what they could divine of this bronze heart. The King of France was less perspicacious. Don Cesare had helped him rid himself of his wife, the saintly Madame Jeanne of France. He had made it equally possible for him to marry the widow of his predecessor, the heiress of Brittany. For this double service, he became Duke of Valentinois, captain of an artillery company, and husband of the sister of the King of Navarre. This man of vaulting ambition possessed all the gifts of nature. Handsome, strong, cunning, fierce, his intelligence was immoderate. Politics did not absorb him; he was a judge of painting, sculpture, architecture and music: he rivalled Duke Alphonso of Ferrara as an

engineer and excellent artilleryman. He
did not know everything, but he knew
about everything, save scruple. When he
saw that he was as great a lord as his birth,
the favor of the Pope, the support of the
King, his marriage, his duchy, and his
company of French gendarmes could make
him, he did not hesitate; he sought whatever property of others was to his liking,
and at one stroke laid his hand on the
Romagna, despoiling, driving out and
terrifying the possessors of cities and
seigniories: those that he caught, he
killed; and, as it was no more for him than
the Romagna, he seized the duchy of
Urbino, whose master, Guidobaldo, was
fortunate enough to take flight in time.
He was already asking himself what might
be his next booty, when the Italian
princes began to remonstrate with Louis
XII at the danger of such a favorite.

Louis XII was astonished; he examined
what they told him; he became anxious.
But he was in the power of his prime minis-

ter; and Cardinal d'Amboise, infatuated with the passion to succeed Alexander as Pope, had need of Don Cesare. The minister palliated matters, denied what he could, was obliged to admit as facts a number of misdeeds, cruelties, perfidies, disquieting and captious dealings, for Don Cesare, thoroughly French as he was, was still negotiating with the enemy and had his finger in various pies that were being served on quite different tables; but, in fine, the Cardinal concluded in favor of his confidant; he disquieted his master and then pacified him. Warned of what was going on, the Duke of Romagna hastened to Milan where the King was. He laughed at the reproaches directed against him, pleaded, protested, swore, flew into a passion. . . . Perhaps he wept; he caressed, he insinuated, he remonstrated, he grew tender, he became touching. . . . He brought into play all the thousand tortuous, unctuous, gentle, gripping coils of his nature, all his brilliant colors; and

these dumbfounded the uncrafty and ill‾
balanced mind of the French king. Cesare
reëstablished his affairs in the best possible
order, and proved that since he was the
indispensable friend of his Most Christian
Majesty he should be trusted; but while
the King and the cardinal minister were
thus doing their best to lift him into
the heaven of success, the earth suddenly
yawned beneath his feet. Something happened to him that was almost worse than
desertion by Louis XII; his troops muti-
nied. Their captains, men quite as covet-
ous as Don Cesare though doubtless
less gifted for command—but blind as to
their own incapacities and clearsighted
regarding their desires—were weary of
being used in his cold hands as instru-
ments that would be broken after serving
their purpose. They planned to seize for
themselves what they had seized for him,
of which they had not been given sufficient
share. They alone conducted his military
forces; but they took no heed of the fact

that they enjoyed political power only
through him, by means of his inventions,
his machinations, and his will, superior to
all the genius that they could command
together. So they resolved to cast down
their leader and possess themselves of his
vacant place. Assailed by his own people,
what could Cesare do? He found himself
opposed by populations that had been
usurped and recently united under his
scepter which was no scepter. What
assistance could he summon? In what
principle of right could he take refuge?
The blow was felling him. Probably King
Louis XII, after granting him his favors as
Duke of Romagna, would find it more
comfortable to have him as a servant.

In this most critical position, Monsieur
de Valentinois did not stop long to calculate. He flung himself into the yawning
abyss. And it is in the depths of that
abyss that we must seek him out and
observe his actions.

PART III
JULIUS II

POPE JULIUS II

Julius II

WHILE Don Cesare Borgia was suffering ruin in Italy, the French, paying the penalty of their mistakes, were losing Gaeta, their last sanctuary on the Neapolitan coast. They began to despair of their most unhappy ambition. Leaving the kingdom to Spain, they concluded with Ferdinand of Aragon a peace that was to end with their lassitude. Meanwhile they felt that their popularity was very feeble. Genoa, occupied since the year 1499, disgusted with them and seething with conspiracies, rose up and drove them out. In Florence, the half-popular, half-aristocratic government, under the hesitating successors of Savonarola, wished them no good. One did not speak of the matter too loudly, but since the Pisa affair, in which

the discernment of Charles VIII had not
played a brilliant rôle, the Florentines had
little use for an ally who supported their
rebellious subjects against them and who
spoke so readily of financial contributions.
In these embarrassing times, one had no
love for needy friends.   There was enough
work to be done already in conciliating the
great lords and the people.   With a secret
terror, men fixed their eyes on the wall
whence passed and repassed the shadow of
the Medici, quite ready to reassume their
power: no one was ignorant of the possibility, many persons desired it; and Pier
Soderini, the perpetual gonfalonier, impotent doctrinaire, had little time in which to
serve Louis XII, when, from morn till
eve, he had to reckon with the desires of an
old people who were in love, he said, with
political agitation, but who were led by the
state of their manners to an ignoble repose,
which was precisely what the Medici
promised.

Meanwhile, the Most Christian King,

despoiled of his pretensions to Naples, was clinging all the more' strongly to his Milanese ideas. In order to give them rein, he entered into negotiations, he called to him the forces that he could command, and to his great joy he succeeded in concluding, on the tenth of December, 1508, the League of Cambray, directed against the Venetians, in which joined Pope Julius II, Ferdinand of Aragon, the Emperor Maximilian, the Dukes of Savoy and Ferrara, and the Marquis of Mantua. It was stipulated that the Holy Father should recover the cities of the Romagna, rescued by Saint Mark from the spoils of Cesare Borgia; that the Emperor should have Verona, Vicenza, Padua, and other lesser places including Friuli; while the Catholic King was to take possession of Trani, Brindisi, Otranto, and Monopoli; and France was to get Bergamo, Brescia and Cremona, old dismembered portions of the Milanese territory. These claims were calculated to strip the Republic of those regions of dry land which, with so much effort, such great cost, and so much skill, she had succeeded in grouping around her lagoons.

Louis XII, overjoyed, began the campaign with the usual impetuosity of the French. He flung himself upon the coveted provinces, pounced upon the Venetian army and gave it a sound thrashing at Agnadello. It was a brilliant triumph. It was gained over one of the greatest warriors of that day, the Orsini, Bartolomeo d'Alviano, a soldier of great bravery and genius.

But while the royal armies were thus working miracles, the imperial armies were ill comporting themselves. The presence of Maximilian did not inspire them. Their movements were dilatory, and the Venetians, excited instead of being cast down by their disaster, bravely recaptured Padua, compelling the Emperor to retreat and driving his troops from Vicenza. Their adversary, who entertained the most exalted ideas of his grandeur, was accustomed to live in a state of theoretical heroism and practical supineness that were constantly parallel: to surround himself by the brilliant splendors beloved of his imagination, he needed money; he did not have it, and this was the great bane of his life and the cause of many actions ill matched to his sublime pretensions. On this occasion, in the midst of his defeats, and while he was being harried out of Italy by the Venetians, he had the consolation of filling his treasury. For the sum of 150,000 ducats paid him by Louis XII, he accorded to this ally the imperial investiture of Milan, and then took his leave. This was the end of his assistance.

On the other hand, the Pope, who now held the Romagna, could no longer see any use in the French alliance; so he brusquely repudiated it and, joining forces with the Venetians, attacked the French; while, in his turn, the Catholic King, satisfied as was Julius II, imitated the example

of the Holy Father. Excepting the Dukes
of Ferrara and Savoy, all Italy now found
itself opposed to Louis XII. The League
of Cambray was turned about. But it
was not enough for the Pope that he put
his ally of yesterday in such danger. He
wished to deal him so severe a blow that
the French would be definitely driven
out of Italy, and never be able to return.
He enticed Henry VIII of England into
the new League, which he called Holy.
Henry was to serve the common cause
by menacing the coasts of Brittany, Nor-
mandy, Gascony, and by sending out bands
of pillagers from the walls of Calais to
overrun the Picard plains. It was a bold
conception, and one that singularly wid-
ened the horizon of political action. In
the same spirit, Julius II had stirred the
Swiss cantons into action through the
intermediation of his favorite, Cardinal
de Sion, a man of great courage, great
obstinacy, and great brutality. He had
promised the mountaineers an enormous

wage and the pillage of the Milanese.
Carried away by enthusiasm, these fighting
men immediately descended from their
heights in dense bands. And with hal-
berds on shoulder, and great two-handed
swords on back, this irresistible infantry
debouched through the defiles of Valtellina
and proclaimed their holy determination
that the cause of the Church should not be
jeopardized.

At the first breath of this tempest,
Louis XII stiffened with admirable valor.
He hurled troops into the Romagna; he
announced that Julius II, a pontiff unworthy the tiara, should be deprived of it;
and to proceed to judgment, in harmony
with the Emperor, he caused a council to
be convoked at Pisa. It seemed that the
deposition of Guliano della Rovere was
assured. At the same time, the King's
nephew, Gaston de Foix, Duke of Nemours,
who was then very young, being only
twenty-four, was parading his triumphant
flags from place to place, and by his con-

sidered audacity, his quick and sure conceptions, and his incomparable activity
was astonishing Europe and compelling its
admiration for so precocious a warrior
genius. He was one of those Dioscuri
who shone in the heaven of the House of
France, the other being the great Condé.
For Nemours at least the comparison is
only too exact; he disappeared like a
shooting star; he died young like the
brother of Pollux, the victory of Ravenna
engulfed him. From this moment all
went ill for Louis XII.

With one hero the less at his side, he
found himself face to face with his indefatigable and implacable pontiff, the
man who halted neither in good nor evil
fortune, whose eyes, hands and mind were
steadily directed toward the execution
of his plans. Julius II succeeded in
pressing the Emperor so closely that he
won him over and made him reverse his
position. Maximilian abandoned Louis
XII, declared that he had forfeited the

Milanese, and restored the duchy to the
Sforzas. The French were obliged to get
out. It was a rout. Genoa, retaken,
revolted; Parma and Placenza placed
themselves under the dominion of the
Pope; the sorry council of Pisa whose
ridiculous authority some poor fugitive
cardinals had tried vainly to establish,
that miserable conventicle that had to
be protectively shepherded as far as
Milan in order to escape the taunts,
insults and missiles of the Pisan populace,
that troublesome group of theologians,
took flight with the cohorts of Louis XII
across the plains of upper Italy. Among
the fugitives, but with an attitude very
different from theirs, a captive but greatly
venerated, went the legate of Julius II, who
had been taken prisoner at Ravenna, that
Giovanni de' Medici who was one day to
be Leo X. The French had been far from
the last to mock the fathers of their council;
in those times they were inclined by nature
to oppose themselves, and consequently,

while hastening toward their frontier, they amused themselves by praising to the skies the cardinal whom their King was planning to imprison closely in France. This hope was frustrated, for in the confusion of a disordered flight the prisoner escaped. He returned to the Pope who was dealing redoubled blows against the last partisans of France. In vain the Duke of Ferrara had turned against the supporters of his House; Julius II wished to exterminate him, and besides he intended to unite the domains of the House of Este to the already perceptibly enlarged patrimony of Saint Peter. As for the Florentines, they had made ill use of the fortune that had given them Pisa, by permitting the French council to convene there. The Pope was the less ready to pardon them because he had inherited the hopes of Cesare Borgia regarding Tuscany. Consequently he turned Don Raymond de Cardona and the Spanish army against the Florentine mercenaries. Meanwhile, Maximilian Sforza,

the son of Ludovico il Moro, having
reëntered Milan, was installed in the city,
and, gripped in the vise of Swiss protection,
he had given to the small cantons Lugano,
Mendrisio and other places situated on the
upper course of the Ticino, while he had
abandoned Bormio and Chiavenna to the
Grisons Confederations. The Swiss, satisfied, finally released their ward. There
still remained some handfuls of French
abandoned here and there in various
strongholds.

When one considers the state of their
own country at this time, it seems that
nothing could have been more fatal for the
French than their passion for descents
into Italy. Guienne, acquired as recently
as 1453, was not yet very affectionate.
For centuries this province had administered its own affairs under an English
protectorate; it had lived with few con-
straints, had payed few taxes, and the new
régime seemed onerous to it. This régime
taught it to give much, and to see itself

checked and handled with a tight rein in a
thousand ways by the servants of the
King. The Aquitainians also were sedi-
tious. Then, too, the kingdom did not
possess Roussillon; it had won Provence,
but the Dauphinate was only annexed and
not consolidated; while the *comté* of Bour-
gogne, Artois, and Flanders no more formed
a part of the monarchy than did Lorraine
or the three bishoprics of Metz, Toul and
Verdun. Calais and its territory remained
in the hands of England, and hampered
the movements and breathing of the
north-western region. Brittany, in separate and independent state, attached to the
crown by marriage, was jealous of the con-
joint power. Let one look at the map
and it will not take him long to be con-
vinced of the truth that France could have
been better occupied than in annexing the
Milanese, even if one wishes to judge
matters only from the strictly practical
viewpoint of temporary interests.

The historians have been so struck by

this truth that the greater number of them
seek in minute causes the determining
reason for what seems to them folly.   It
has been said that in the reign of Charles
VIII it was the adventurous spirit of the
King alone that put France on the march.
Under Louis XII, writers have seen in the
same action the personal interests of Cardinal d'Amboise, employing in the service
of his fantastic papal ambitions the excessive authority of which the weakness of his
monarch made him the depositary.

In thus analyzing things one explains,
indeed, how the still feeble resources of
the kingdom came to be expended in badly
planned enterprises that led the French
troops into the peninsula only to make
them soon come out again in a more or less
unfortunate manner.   By court intrigues
one can equally explain how it was that
military chiefs and administrators of countries so precariously conquered were usu-
ally unfitted for the functions confided to
them; and, finally, one can explain the acts

of violence, the exactions, the malpractices, and the clumsiness which resulted in disaster.

But what remains unexplained is the general predilection for expeditions into Italy, which was common at this time not only in France but also in Germany and in Spain. In all these countries, immediate and daily interests should equally have opposed the universal disposition to turn away from local questions for the sake of adventuring in the peninsula. Indeed, everyone was flocking in that direction: Picards and Saxons, Castilians and Swiss. Yet they had many other things to do, and they were doing them. Cardinal Ximemes was employing the revenues of his archbishopric of Toledo, the richest in the world, in hiring troops that he led in person to the siege of Oran; Alphonso D'Albuquerque was staking Portuguese chances on the East Indian seas, and was founding at Goa an empire stretching from the Arabian sea to the shores of China.

As for Germany, rich, learned, and capable of local freedom, it was gravitating toward Italy in just the same fashion as were France, Portugal and Spain. It is quite true that these countries dreamed only of gratifying their ambitions, and that the courtiers thought only of fortune's chances, but underneath these individual motives there was another motive, powerful in quite another way: the one that was setting in motion the spirit of the age. There can be no doubt about it: men were instinctively seeking the intellectual light where it was to be found. They felt vaguely, but at least they felt, this interest of primary importance, and they worked in such a way as to satisfy it. They did not explain very clearly to themselves what they wished of Italy; generally they were mistaken as to what they were going to ask of her; she herself made a greater mistake than her assailants, in supposing that she had the power to attract and to repulse them at will; but it is none the less

true that the future of the world's intellectual development demanded that a
general drawing together take place, and it
did take place, not because Italy was
constrained to give some one of her members to each of these foreigners who wished
to tear her in pieces, but because she
inoculated all of them with something of
her genius. The whole process of uncon-
scious gravitation, the manner in which
intellectual influences and emanations
spread, is assuredly one of the strongest
demonstrations of the existence of those
mysterious laws which, at certain moments, act upon the development of mankind, in precisely the same fashion that
these same laws, in an organic application,
operate upon the growth and coloration of
bodies.

The hero of this period, included between
the dates 1503 and 1513, is Julius II. In
this exceedingly complex whole, so alive
with deep-rooted and animated fibers,
Julius II, Guliano della Rovere, repre-

sents most completely and most forcefully
the energetic fiber. In the general seething, he seethed more than any other. His
entire life was an irritated appetence for action and creation. In this age when everyone saw things in the large his vision was
as great as anyone's, and he turned his
active hands to the production of the vast-
est realities. Scrupulous he was not; but
who was? He had passed the years of his
youth and his maturity in seeking the
means of omnipotence so that he might
execute the ideas which filled his head and
swelled his heart. Even while he was
defending his life against Alexander VI,
he had ceaselessly plunged again and again
into the mines and countermines necessary to open a way to the pontifical throne.
He had deceived, duped and tricked
Cardinal d'Amboise and many another.
Woe to those who barred his road. Yet,
by comparison, he was not considered
vicious: he was too imposing. Men did
not entrust themselves to him, and they

would have been mistaken to abandon themselves to him; yet they recognized that the elevation of his ideas, which in many respects made him touch the sublime, filled this singular soul with a savage generosity. The fact that in his court the glory of the Holy See came before the glory of his family, made him more useful than his predecessors; and the glory of Italy, closely united in his mind to the glory of the Church, should eternally recommend his memory to those who hold patriotism as the first of virtues. So soon as a fact appeared exalted to him, it pleased him, he comprehended it; and thus it is that this haughty and turbulent pontiff was assuredly the most effective among the protectors of the arts, just as the time in which he reigned was the true period of expansion of the genius of the Renaissance.

PART IV

LEO X

Leo X

THE physiognomy of Cardinal Giovanni de' Medici, the future Pope Leo X, is one of the first to be distinguished from the faces of the Middle Age. Ere long, Francis I and Charles V place themselves at his side; they differ no less than he from the men of the preceding generation; but he is the herald, he announces the modern epoch. One sees in him manners that are elegant and no longer passionate; to these he joins the charm of comparative simplicity and moderation; his scruples are not extraordinary, yet he appreciates the value of apparent mildness. His faith is slight, but he scarcely ever departs from an approximate propriety; he is never preoccupied with great works, with great institutions destined to produce good, yet in smaller ways he enjoys the pleasure of beneficence: he takes pleasure in endowing poor children. He is not at all handsome; he has noble manners and delicate habits; his large, bulging eyes do not permit him to recognize objects easily, which causes him to appreciate the virtues of the eyeglass and to show how it may be used gracefully. He is fat and subject to violent fits of perspiration which embarrass him excessively. His lymphatic temperament causes him even graver inconveniences, and during the conclave from which he emerged Pope he was obliged to submit to surgical operations; but he has hands that are white, long, plump and admirable, and by the propriety of his gestures he knows how to make the most of them. A hundred years before, even fifty, all these minor facts would not have been recorded.

So early an event as his birth was one of them. He gave himself out for a prince, and, ordinarily, no one contradicted him.

POPE LEO X

It was, however, a fiction. His father Lorenzo the Magnificent, enjoyed no other position than that of an opulent citizen whose political virtues and exquisite taste in all things well served his ambition. Nothing more. The family blood was the blood of the counting house; the least gentleman of feudal origin would not have admitted equality with this merchant race, yet nevertheless, after the revolution of Savonarola, these sons of exiled Florentine traders, along with many others, made themselves accepted as being of superior blood for the unique reason that they pretended to be; men thought that they were apt to reign some day, because they vaguely felt that Florence was drifting toward monarchy. Such an admission on the part of general opinion was no less novel than the personality of Cardinal Giovanni. Its first result was that, in the same way that a ripe fruit detaches itself from the branch without which it could never have become a fruit, so the

Medici detached themselves from their wealth which had made them what they were, and, though poor, they were still able to remain important. Piero de' Medici, hunted from his native city, found himself with his brothers and kinsmen journeying, wandering, drifting, begging and being rebuffed, from Bologna to Venice, from Venice into Germany, from Germany into France. Men sometimes mocked him and his followers, they refused to support them, they refused to aid them; they often lacked the bare necessities of life and were compelled to quit inns where they could obtain no credit. Yet no one questioned the fact that they were princes, and this point alone sufficed to reserve the future for them.

Piero, who succeeded Lorenzo as head of the family, was from all points of view a mediocre man. It was not this, however, that was responsible for his downfall. It was the natural reaction against the mode of administration introduced by his family.

The Florentine temperament, like that of
all peoples, was complex. Instincts hostile
to the Medici, which were held in check
under the hand of Lorenzo, were released
under that of his maladroit son. But it
has been justly observed that a government
which exists uniquely on the condition
that it commit no faults, gives proof by
that fact alone of scant vitality. Piero's
power was broken because he encountered
a certain fund of ancient energies that
demanded release, certain illusions that
had to be exhausted.

Everyone felt it: the zeal of Savonarola,
the historic and speculative theories of
Machiavelli and his learned friends, en-
amored of a Roman ideal, the pretensions
to influence of the great families, the balanced and counterbalanced cunning of the
Soderini, the Valori, and their like, more
sagacious than perspicacious, and more
moderate than strong, could neither lead
far nor last for long. The mere fact that
the slightest discomfort of this liberal

régime, whenever felt, made the name of
Medici shine forth, invoked as a panacea
for all ills, was sufficient to give comfort
to the exiles.   But before they could again
lay hands on their advantages, their ill
luck had to run its course.

Piero died. Giovanni became the mentor
of his family.   He let the younger branch
obscurely reënter Florence, change its
name and humble itself, while he continued
slowly and with no false steps in the rôle of
pretender; each day that fled, each new
misery that was felt in the wearied Republic enveloped and supported his name with
a dangerous brilliance.   The Cardinal was
patient, he was at bottom satisfied with his
fate; indubitably he was not slumbering,
but neither was he too wide awake.   Every
day his friends became more numerous.
Tolerantly looked upon by Alexander VI,
but careful not to reside at Rome under the
hand of that terrible personage, he
entered into relations with the declared
enemy of the Pope, the mettlesome Guliano

della Rovere. This man was fortified in his episcopal city of Ostia, and was moving heaven and earth to effect the deposition of Borgia. The elegant Giovanni de' Medici met him at Savona, in a premeditated interview. They conversed for a long time. Doubtless Guliano proposed many schemes, for never was there a more active or fertile genius than his; he suggested many overtures, he displayed the possibility of many violent acts that would hurl the abhorred pontiff to the earth. But Giovanni de' Medici was not the man to be tempted·thus, and the interview at Savona was productive of nothing that might have given Alexander VI cause for complaint. At the same time, the two interlocutors parted friends. It is difficult enough to imagine what sort of sympathy the rather cold temperament, curt reason and intellectual refinement of the Medici could have excited in the most impetuous and at the same time most cunning of men; yet this sympathy existed, and was even destined to develop considerable proportions when Julius had assumed the tiara.

At the moment, the Cardinal, having returned from the last of his ultramontane journeys, after having seen much, learned much, conversed with many scholars, and admired a host of art objects, gave himself up to a dilettantism which had become, since the time of Lorenzo the Magnificent, the obligatory and the justified pretension of his family. Seconded by his cousin, Cardinal Giulio, later Clement VII, he had converted his house into a museum. There one could converse with the finest and most amiable spirits of the age; there one met the people who were taking leading parts in the most important affairs. Amid such disinterested pleasures, Giovanni de' Medici always kept a part of his attention fixed on the political fluctuations, through which might be glimpsed as a probability the reintegration of his family at Florence and the recovery of what that family called its rights.

On this point Giovanni came to no understanding with Julius II. The Pope was willing that the Medici should retrieve their confiscated domains and a certain rank, but not that they should become reigning princes. Himself, as we have seen, coveted Tuscany, and envisaged the inclusion of this region in the great pontifical Italy whose creation he was attempting; and even had he felt much more good will than he did toward Giovanni, he would not have turned aside from his projects. So he readily made the Cardinal his commissioner to the Venetians and Spaniards marching with his troops against the French; he initiated him into his intrigues; and, when he saw him taken prisoner at Milan after Ravenna, he employed him to institute the Lateran council destined to react against Louis XII and the Emperor who had turned theologians at Pisa: but when he attacked Florence, if he again made use of him, he placed him, as we have seen, under the

double guardianship of the Duke d'Arbois
and Don Raymond de Cardona. So the
Medici understood perfectly well that
the extreme limit of his favor had been
reached, that the Holy Father would
thenceforward look upon him with eyes
of suspicion, and that he had either to
submit absolutely, abandon Tuscany to the
representative of Saint Peter and not make
a wry face over it, or definitely recommence
a battle; indeed, there was no other way to
keep one's footing against such an adversary as Julius II.

Rarely does man foresee events accu-
rately. His reason is no more than an
unreason constantly reversed by the course
of facts over which it has no control.
Julius II dies suddenly, and Cardinal
Giovanni, the suspected confidant, the
man held in check, the pretender, on the
eve of losing all, finds himself sovereign
pontiff, possessed of the forces that have
been turned against him. At this moment
Leo X entered into the full possession of

his temperament: unimpeded he became the magnificent seigneur that he really was, the prince, the man of passions more colorful then strong. He realized the ideal of a perfectly ornate existence.

His political sentiments had little of the Italian in them, and what he sought was not the sudden elevation of his family after the fashion of the Borgias, but, following him, the right of his House to the principality of its natal city. Further, he imagined that he could create the semblance of a State for his brother Giuliano by uniting to Parma and Placentia, remnants of the House of Este, Modena, purchased from the Emperor for forty thousand gold ducats (the Emperor asked only to sell). Francis I having mounted the throne of France, the Pope transferred to him the species of hate that he had dedicated to Louis XII. However, when he saw that young conqueror reënter the Milanese, through the exploit of Marignano, drive out the Sforzas with a

like Augustus, he desired stagnation with
severity. The Pope, without perhaps realizing it clearly, was abandoning the idea
of Italian unity and preponderance; he
preferred many things to the grandeur of
the Church; and the Emperor readily
consented to the elevation of a few more
princes, even Medici, if at this price he
became master in the peninsula and drove
out the French. Nothing either in the
Emperor or in the Pope resembled what
men had been familiar with some years
before. Moreover, Italy, rich, admired,
learned, inspired and skilful, was weary;
fatigue was invading her; passion was
waning; indolence was spreading; men
laughed while despairing, and, laughing,
they despaired. Everyone followed the
Pope, men believed less and less in religion
and in everything else. The enthusiasms
of the past were slowly but surely transforming themselves into dilettantism.
Foreigners, too, the old pillagers, were
turning artists. Throughout Europe,

thenceforward, the value of beautiful
things was appreciated well or ill. Princes
hold themselves in honor bound to seek
them out. Francis I orders immense
purchases of art works; Henry VIII, the
devoted friend and servant of the Holy See,
piques himself on doing as much: Charles
Fifth imitates them.

And meanwhile the world is using its
wits, struggling, and bestirring itself.
In Germany arise innovators of all kinds;
they are making their pens run actively
and already baring their swords to the
breeze; printers go from city to city with
their apprentices and their presses, sowing
pamphlets, libels, tracts, discourses, warnings and exhortations, sometimes catholic,
sometimes heretical, but kindling the fire
everywhere; the populace develop a liking
for this first form of journalism; Erasmus
and Reuchlin, in their scholars' studies,
speculate on the notions of the day, and
carry on correspondence with kings, who
are flattered to receive letters that are

printed, and who ask advice with the reservation that they shall not follow it. The intellectual conflagration is general. It has penetrated France; its results are making themselves felt over the whole globe: Magellan discovers his strait and dies in the Philippines; Hernando Cortez, the great Marquis accomplishes the conquest of Mexico in thirty months. Men's minds are all aflame, but combustibles are soon to be lacking.

It is at the apogee of things that one may, with some effort of research, discover the hatching of the germ of their decay. At precisely this moment, superficial minds are least disposed to suspect such a thing. They slumber in a complete security; they are almost ready to believe that the eternal law, by virtue of which all things are dedicated to transformation through death, has ceased to operate. The years before them are numbered and few; yet they calculate on indefinite centuries. Everything excuses them: the air is sweet, warm, perfumed; the sky, freed of morning mists, is of incomparable purity, and the chariot of the sun mounts calmly to the zenith of its course, its golden wheels illumining the blue. Only, the guide of the sublime coursers has changed: it is no longer Phœbus, it is Phaeton.

PART V

MICHAEL ANGELO

MICHELANGELO BUONARROTI

Michael Angelo

COMING after Leo X, Adrian of
Utrecht was resolved to exercise the
ecclesiastical power in accordance with the
spirit of Christian dogma: he desired
neither beautiful antiquity, nor arts, nor
luxury; he had no liking for evil manners,
and clerical corruption felt the smart of
the rods with which he was armed. Were
the strayed sheep going to reënter the
proper fold? There is reason to doubt it,
nothing ever returns; but, from all evidence, the intentions of the pontiff were as
upright as they were severe. He mounted
the throne in January, 1522, and on the
24th of December, 1523, he was dead.
During this brief period, the pontifical
court, outraged in its habits, had scarcely
drawn breath. Once it was free, it did

not wish to accept such trials again, and
the cardinals united in conclave raised
to the supreme pontificate Giulio de'
Medici, the pallid image of Leo X, his
bastard brother and a bastard in all
things. He had the same kind of spirit,
with less spirit, the same taste for pleasure,
with less delicacy, the same taste for the
arts, the same taste for letters . . . but it
was only taste. The Italian decadence
has already begun; the petals of the golden
flower are falling one by one. In order
to become too intoxicating, the perfume
loses its freshness. Hereafter everything
happens in an atmosphere of descending
twilight. Events of importance in Italy
are rare and melancholy. A picture of this
period may be given briefly; one is no
longer in the midst of fecund moments,
when two or three years witness the production of the most grandiose movements.

Clement VII reigned in the midst of the
most horrible and fruitless agitations;
after him came Alessandro Farnese, Paul

III, the great amateur of nepotism; but everything was becoming paltry, even the faults: by the abusive gifts of the Popes, the patrimony of the Church was assuredly despoiled and impoverished, but the Pier Luigi Farnesi and the Ottavio Farnesi received only lands, money and titles; they asked no more; vigorous ambitions, having ceased to be useful, no longer existed; contemporary conditions made them no longer possible. Julius III succeeded Paul III, Marcellus II preceded Paul IV who was followed by Pius IV. During these reigns the Popes sometimes tried to resist Cæsar, to ally themselves to France, to persecute the friends of Cæsar, to ruin the Colonna, partisans of Cæsar; in fine the authority of Cæsar was steadily augmented, and although Paul IV, in 1556, was bold enough to pronounce the forfeiture of Spain by Philip II, and expel him from the throne of Sicily, he soon had to swallow his words, submit, and once more practise obedience.

Everything bowed to the double will of Spain and the Empire. These powers, directed by the same maxims, by a clear vision of the same interests, exerted a crushing weight on their own domains, and, as far as possible, on those of other princes. Charles Fifth had bequeathed to the two branches of his House a murderous policy which was bound either to ruin those who practised it or to crush the rest of the world. Two ardent spirits confronted each other. One was the spirit of the dying age, pursuing schism, heresy, and the immoderate authority of princes in one direction, and in another indefinite liberty for subjects, the unexpected, the incoherent, the inconsistent, unexplained desire and dreams, and hastening no one knew whither. The other spirit, which inspired the princes of the House of Burgundy, was determined to check, to suppress and to annul everything whatsoever: mistrustful, mischievous, questioning and troublesome, born of the fear that it might lose some fraction of its possessions, its powers, its rights, or its pretensions, it implacably opposed the pretensions, the rights, the powers, the possessions, the very life of all and everyone in the entire universe. It was for the sake of enjoying at home the melancholy peace, which alone he recognized as peace, that Philip II maintained disorder in Italy and in France; and his imperial relatives pursued precisely the same policy in Germany, in Bohemia, and in Hungary.

This age witnessed the reawakening of the passion for propaganda, of which scarcely anything had been heard since the ancient sermons of Christianity. Now two terrible converters arose and set to work; neither the one nor the other has rested down to the present day, and they still implacably pursue recruits. While the one, demon of revolt, preached the future, the other, on the contrary, preached the past, but what past? A past that never was. Philip II, following his father,

revealed himself as an inexorable mission-
ary of the oppression which he insisted
had been the ancient rule, and of which
he and the monk of Yuste were really the
inventors. He sent out his chosen collab-
orators in the most diverse and distant
directions: Inquisitors for the faith and
fathers of Jesus, new militias, who were
sometimes in agreement and often dis-
cordant; here favorable to the Holy See,
there its inspectors, sometimes its enemies.
But at this time and for long afterward,
both the one force and the other were
resolutely imperial, resolutely Spanish.
It would be footless to style them persecutors; that would be to grant them a
monopoly of cruelties, and in these their
adversaries showed themselves quite as
skilful.   It was no less perilous to have
dealings with the ecclesiastical judges of
Henry VIII or with the Calvinists
of Geneva than with the Dominicans of
Cordova.   All parties have been, are, and
will be persecutors; all parties have called

their impositions justice, and have stamped
as cruelty what they have been forced to
submit to; but the passions of Philip II
were nobler than those of Henry VIII.

The remarkable point is that the Christian religion—which furnished standards
for all camps, and which loaned its name in
Saxony, in Sweden, and in England, as in
Madrid, Vienna, Naples and Brussels—
this Christian religion of which men spoke
so much, was actually little heeded. In
the days of ancient Greece a war broke
out which was the source of much misery:
it is known in history under the name of
the "Sacred War," and it arose over the
sanctuary of Delphi. Had someone
among the Hellenes denied the divinity
of Phœbus Apollo? Had someone dared
to alter a rite, omit a ceremony? Had the
veracity of the Sibyl been questioned?
Nothing less! They pillaged pilgrims and,
perhaps, the temple itself somewhat; that
is what rendered this war sacred. The
religious dissensions of modern Europe

are of the same kind. Through the faith
they aim at the most practical interests,
at interests in which the immortal soul
cannot claim the least part. Hence the
thousand contradictions, the bizarre fea-
tures, the inconsistencies of religious politics; hence the rejection of the Spanish
Inquisition by the Popes, even though this
Inquisition was, so to speak, the buckler
of orthodoxy; hence the Popes offended,
insulted, persecuted, driven from Rome,
reduced to misery, to starvation,—and
by whom? By Charles Fifth; then vili-
fied again by Philip II, by those Catholic
monarchs who were indignant at not finding in the will of the Holy Father either
the measure, the precise shade, or the
form of Catholicism which was suited to
their own affairs, I insist temporal affairs.
The same causes were at work a little later
in France, when the House of Guise and
the League accused the Papacy of luke-
warmness, and when, in this same country,
Louis XIV, the flail of heresy, humiliated

the Sovereign Pontiff as completely as
possible, and ordained that the clergy
in his States should be placed under the
absolute control of his administration.
In opposition to the dogmatic rigidity of
the potentates, the court of Rome, from the
sixteenth century onward, showed itself
lenient in the matter of faith. It made
its reservations on occasion, it determined
its doctrines theoretically and defined the
extent of its rights; but it insisted much less
on practice, and seemed even, in many
cases, to desire to live without any colli·
sions with heterodoxy. In consequence, it
came about that as the Protestant powers
promptly imitated the rigor of the Catholic
governments, religious persecutions more
and more laid aside the character of faithful fanaticism, to assume more positively
that of State expedience. Down to the
present time these confessional disguises
have continued to mask the most
absolutely temporal aims.

Charles Fifth made his fashion of

envisaging religion his principal business, his great power. Armed with an inflexible constancy, he waged war against all who opposed themselves to the perpetration of his wishes. As Francis I was his chief adversary, he made it his task to close Italy to him. He succeeded. But it was not the work of a single day. In 1523, he drove him out of the Milanese and pursued him into Provence; but he was repulsed and compelled to turn back on his tracks before a new invasion led by the King in person. In 1524, at Pavia, he defeated his adversary, took him prisoner, and carried him to Madrid. In 1526, constrained to release him, he had to content himself with an inexecutable treaty. In 1527, the French, allied with the Pope, Florence, the Venetians, the Swiss and England, reappeared in the peninsula without any resultant profit; however, they penetrated as far as Naples, again lost that kingdom in 1528, and again consented to evacuate it. In 1529, the Ladies'

Peace was signed at Cambray, negotiated by Marguerite of Austria, mistress of the Low Countries, and Louise of Savoy. The French solemnly renounced all possessions in Italy and any interference in that country whatsoever, and, as corollary and confirmation of this absolute defeat, the peninsular States formed a perpetual league under the protection and leadership of the Emperor. So this was arranged in complete accordance with his designs. In 1530, he caused the iron crown and the imperial crown to be bestowed on him by Clement VII, his victim. He was the master; the Pope was no more than a passive assistant and deacon to the officiating Emperor. Thereafter Cæsar bought himself friends. He made a duchy of the marquisate of Mantua. To the Duke of Ferarra he gave Carpi and promised Modena and Reggio. He besieged Florence for six months, took the city, despite defensive works executed by Michael Angelo, and put an end to the indefinite vacillation of the inhabitants by assigning them a hereditary chief in the person of Alessandro de' Medici; this was a courtesy to the Pope, whom the Emperor did not wish to abuse too far. To his cousin, Beatrice of Savoy, Charles made the gift of the marquisate of Ceva and the *comté* of Asti. Montferrat he gave to the Mantuan. Before long a revolution broke out in Florence, Alessandro was assassinated: no matter. From among the Medici, Cæsar chose Cosimo, a boy of eighteen, son of Giovanni delle Bande Nere, and made him Duke. Sienna revolted and drove out the Spanish garrison. Charles took the city, modified the government, and put the Sienese under the guardianship of a strong citadel. They sought to rise again; they were captured once more, and this time given to Cosimo, Duke of Florence; and as Francesco Burlamacchi, gonfalonier of Lucca was conspiring against the Duke, Cæsar made him prisoner and had him beheaded. At the same time that

he was giving, he was receiving. In 1535,
Francesco Sforza had been reëstablished
in his duchy by the French themselves,
who had then lost their desire for Milan
and who coveted Naples. The Emperor
had allowed him to reign, while keeping
a close watch over him. At his death,
Sforza declared Cæsar his heir.

In this fashion the new constitution of
Italy was definitely established. It was
based on Spanish and imperial supremacy.
The French, indeed, could never desist
from their efforts to bring trouble into the
land. However, they could neither destroy nor establish anything. They continued their old system. It remained easy
for them to enter the peninsula; to main-
tain themselves there was impossible,
and Italy, perpetually trampled under foot
by political schemers, lost even the sentiment of independence. The temperament
of its princes and the habits of its people
became equally servile.

The characteristic feature of this situ-

ation was that the House of Austria understood its own desires, while France seemed
not even to suspect what it wished and ran
to the four winds. It invented the alliance
with the Turk, and it was considered a
stroke of genius. Venice, formerly, had
lived at peace with this power, it had even
tacitly supported it, served it on occasion;
but it had never deemed it wise to make it a
declared friend. France thought of doing
so and boasted of it, which naturally
excited horror in an age when the name
Turk was associated with the mad cruelties exercised on the people of Hungary,
and even Italy, by the janissaries on the
one hand and the Barbary pirates on the
other. At the same time, the councillors
of Francis I. and sequently those of Henry
II, associated themselves with the Protestants because the Emperor was persecut-
ing the latter. When, a little later, they
tortured them no less, they imagined
that it was possible to be friends with
foreign Protestants while they burned

the native breed. This vacillation, too, passed for a masterpiece of wisdom. On the whole, they discovered without examining the matter too closely that it was productive of much evil and very little good, and that it would be more profitable to practice a system that was more respectable from the viewpoint of logic as well as that of morality. Unfortunately this was impossible. Life was hazardous under the Valois, and men were occupied only with fishing in the sea of expedients, the sea of chance prey. The children of Francis I dreamed of absolute power and the destruction of the nobles; the nobles were no longer the feudatories of old, but the products of fortune: the Guises, the Chatillons, the Saint-Andrés. As for them God knows what they desired! Everything! And they awaited the rest. Antithetically to the prayers of kings, they dreamed even of instituting a Republic. They did not dare to confess all that was hatching obscurely in the back of their

minds, so they were reduced to the condition indicated above: they put religion
forward, and remained crouching behind
it.

This method appeared equally excellent
to Henry VIII of England. This prince
had been known as being devoted body and
soul to the court of Rome, and his august
pen had pitted itself so valiantly against
Luther and the reformers that it had been
necessary to give him the title "Defender
of the Faith." He would probably have
continued in the same ways, for the faith,
especially after the manner of Charles
Fifth, could have held nothing for him that
was not most attractive, had he not
unfortunately become acquainted with
Anne Boleyn. After the first step was
hazarded, Catherine of Aragon having been
sent away, the King having been declared
supreme religious head by the Catholic
clergy of his State, the ideas of the theo-
logian of Windsor turned topsy turvy.
So long as he remained Catholic he could

oversee and regulate with a high hand the
orthodoxy of his people, but to create it
was still more agreeable; and massacres
and autos da fe and decapitation of men,
women, children, great lords and poor
wretches, began, to continue for a long
time to come. Catholics, Lutherans, Calvinists, passed the axe from hand to hand
and mounted the same funeral piles; the
important and difficult thing was to guess
the faith of the King, who was uncertain
himself. He was already too busy organiz-
ing the defile of his wives, from Anne Boleyn,
beheaded, to Jane Seymour, who died in
childbirth, to Anne of Cleves, put away,
to Catherine Howard, executed, to Catherine Parr, who would have been, had not
the ingrate Death come to take its pur-
veyor by the throat.

Murder for theological causes flourished
everywhere, in all camps. Everyone
piqued himself on burning well, torturing
well, and it seemed that a doctrine was not
complete so long as it had not erected its

own particular stake. The Anabaptists worked on a grand scale; and they were repaid in-full. The result was that in this age when erudition and the arts should have regulated or at least attracted to themselves mental activity, when, according to generally admitted opinion, the greatest intellectual cultivation should have softened men's manners, men were most particularly cruel, brutal, and blindly fanatical; and in the Protestant countries, for example, trials for sorcery multiplied in a fashion unknown until then, and continued their atrocities until well into the seventeenth century. That is what the great intellectual culture was able to effect, or what it could not prevent.

Human imagination possesses a pharmacopœia from which it draws receipts from time to time. It even has panaceas which reappear periodically. In 1536, men felt that the disorder was at its height and thought that they could not sustain a stronger dose; so they had recourse to the

specific of specifics, and Pope Paul III
convoked a general council. The action of
an assembly is always supposed to give aid
to desperate cases; generally the remedy
kills the patient. The Council of Trent
did not fail to perform the natural function
of assemblies. It killed the religious
unity of Europe, definitely excluded all
living reformers from its communion,
and furnished cause for the appearance of
those who did not yet exist. But it did
not limit itself to this immense mistake.
It discredited the authority that it was
squandering. Among the princes represented at the Council, there were few, if
any, who did not repent either of having been invited or of having accepted.
Abandoned to all the confusion of which a
council is capable, it dragged on for eighteen years; and often it was the Pope,
first of all, who found himself embarrassed
to the point of not knowing what to do.
Suspended in 1547, transferred to Bologna
so that it might be subject to the influence

of the Emperor, interrupted, recontinued in 1551, abandoned the following year, it was not convened again until 1562.

So we see the depths of misery over which the last pictures of the Italian Renaissance unfold themselves: no longer is there any brilliancy, no longer any purity.